Excel for Business:

"The Simplest Way to Enter the Rich World of the Calc Spreadsheet"

"Strategic Use of the Calc Spreadsheet in Business Environments.
Data Analysis and Business Modeling"

Author
Francesco Iannello

Table of Contents

EXTRA BONUS

Excel for Everyone:

The Simplest Way to Enter the Rich World of the Calc Spreadsheet

Author
Francesco Iannello

The following information is presented purely for informative purposes and is therefore considered universal. The information presented within is done so without a contract or any other type of assurance as to its quality or validity.

Any trademarks which are used are done so without consent and any use of the same does not imply consent or permission was gained from the owner. Any trademarks or brands found within are purely used for clarification purposes and no owners are in anyway affiliated with this work.

Introduction Excel for Everyone

I want to thank you and congratulate you for purchasing *Excel for Everyone: The Simplest Way to Enter the Rich World of the Calc Spreadsheet.* Microsoft Excel is one of the most commonly neglected programs that nearly everyone owns or has access to. By purchasing this book, you are now on your way to saving time and energy by easily completing a wide variety of common tasks with the help of this ubiquitous program. As you begin to work with Excel regularly there are a number of actions and required steps that may seem strange or even arcane at first. It is important to persevere, however, as proper Excel use is a skill, which means that like any other skill the only way to improve is to practice as frequently and repeatedly as possible.

This book contains proven steps and strategies designed to ensure you get the most out of every interaction you have with Excel. Inside you will learn the basic purposes of the program and how it can help you be more effective in a number of different ways. From there you will learn about the primary ways to interact with Excel, how to sort and filter complex data, how to use formulas and functions effectively, how to print and create graphs and how to understand common error messages and how to avoid them.

Thanks again for purchasing this book, I hope you enjoy it!

Chapter 1: Understanding Excel

Once you understand what is required, using Excel can provide you a wide variety of options when it comes to working with data in a multitude of forms. One of the primary ways to use Excel is most often associated with the financial sector and allows the user to create their own formulas and then use them to calculate everything from an annual report to a simple sales forecast. It can also be used for a variety of tracking and organizational purposes such as creating status reports, contact lists, invoicing and nearly anything else you could ever need. It can also come in handy when it comes to dealing with large sets of complex numbers which may require charting, graphing or statistical analysis.

Excel groups related data into workbooks with each workbook then containing numerous worksheets dedicated to specific tasks and functions. Each workbook and worksheet is completely customizable and can be interacted with and manipulated in a number of ways. Data is stored in a mixture of vertical and horizontal rows with each row and column then being broken down even further into individual cells. Get used to the cells, they are the primary method of interacting with the spreadsheet. Each cell can store either letters or numbers but it is best to generally stick with one or the other as many sorting functions can only search for one type of character at a time.

Each cell can then be attached to additional cells through the use of what are known as formulas. Formulas can be created on the fly or users have the option of applying numerous formulas that come premade. Preprogrammed formulas include things like finding the standard deviation, common mathematical formulas and even calculate interest payments. Each cell also has the ability to use a formula and then display the results based on a variety of criteria. Cells can also be colored uniquely as well as given unique fonts, borders and more.

When it comes to creating charts and graphs, Excel offers up many more options than a simple word processing program can. Excel can translate data into a wide variety of form from a diverse multipoint pivot chart to the classic pie chart, if you know where to look, Excel does it all.

This also makes Excel a natural choice when you are looking to identify trends in what may otherwise seem like meaningless data. It also makes a numerous additional variables much easier to view on the fly. The easy ability you will have when it comes to manipulating variables will make predicting future patterns easier than you ever thought possible.

This is in part because of the way that you can use Excel to bring disparate points of data together through the use of workbooks and interconnected worksheets. Essentially, what it all boils down to is that if you are not regularly using a spreadsheet to make your life easier, you are working harder, not smarter.

Chapter 2: Primary Interactions with the Excel

When you first start up Excel, you most likely opened up a new worksheet. This new worksheet automatically spawns a new workbook and two additional worksheets for you to switch between, specifics for worksheet management will be discussed later. On the new worksheet screen you will notice that the columns are labeled A, B, C etc. while the rows are labeled 1, 2, 3, 4, etc. Combing the two for a specific cell gives that cell its unique cell reference. Cell references can then be used to indicate to other cells that they need to refer back to the cell with that specific reference. This is what is known as a formula and a basic example is written thusly: =B4+A9

A cell's individual reference is always listed in what is known as the Name Box when that cell is selected. The name box can be found in the top left of the screen, directly below the Home Tab. To the immediate right of the name box is what is known as the Formula Bar. If the selected cell contains information, it will be displayed in the formula bar.

Interacting with cells
Choosing cells
- You can select individual cells by left clicking on them with your mouse or by using the arrow keys.

- If you push the ENTER key the cell directly beneath the cell which is currently selected will become selected. This can be changed by selecting the File tab, then choosing Options and Advanced Options. From there, choose Edit and then the option labeled Enter Move Selection, this will let you determine what direction the selection cursor will move when ENTER is pressed.

- Pressing the TAB key will select the cell to the right of the cell which is currently selected.

- If you wish to select an entirety of a column or row, left click on the row or column in question.

- If you wish to select a group of cells that are next to one another, left click on the first cell you wish to select and drag the cursor to the final cell you wish to select. The selected cells will be shown in black.

- If you wish to select a group of cells that are not next to one another, left click on the first cell you wish to select while at the same time holding down the CTRL key, click on each cell you wish to select while continuing to hold down the CTRL key.

- If you wish to select the entirety of the current worksheet, click on the space between the label for A and the label for 1.

Adding information to cells
- Information can be added to any cell by simply left clicking on it and then entering the required data.

- You can edit the data in any cell by first selecting the cell and then editing the information in the formula bar. Clicking on a different cell or pressing the ENTER key will save the changes.

- If you wish to edit the information in a given cell in the cell directly, simply double click the left mouse button to show the entirety of the data. This can also be accomplished by left clicking once and then pressing the F2 key.

Copying information between cells
- If you wish to copy the data from a cell to the cell or cells below it, simply select the cell with the required data as well as the cell below it and press the CTRL key in conjunction with the D key.

- If you wish to copy the data from a cell to the cell or cells to the left of it simply select the cell with the required data as well as the cell or cells to the left of it and pressing the CTRL key in conjunction with the R key.

- In addition to these handy time savers, the information in any cell can be added to any other cell with the use of what is known as the Fill Handle. Start by selecting the cell with the data to be copied before moving your cursor to the lower right corner of the cell until the cursor changes shape. Now simply select the cell or cells that the data should be copied to.

- If the data to be copied is either one in a series, a unit of time or a date the fill option will include the next logical part of the sequence in each subsequent cell. For example, using the fill option on a cell filled with Monday would make the next box Tuesday, then Wednesday etc.

- To copy a cell and all of its data completely, select the cell in question before right-clicking on it and selecting the copy option. The cut option and the paste option will also work as expected.

Adding a date or time to a cell
- Start by selecting the cell you wish to add data to

- To include a specific date, add the date to the cell as either 1/2/33 or 1-Feb-1933.

- To enter a specific time in the second half of the day write it as 1:00 p as Excel assumes times all times are A.M. unless told otherwise.

- The current time and date can be added to any cell by pressing the SHIFT key in conjunction with the CTRL key and the SEMICOLON key.

- To make a specific cell always display the current time add NOW to it and press enter.

- To make a specific cell always display the current date type TODAY and press enter.

- To determine the default way the time and date are determined press the SHIFT key in conjunction with the CTRL key and the 2 key to bring up the Regional and Languages menu and select the settings you prefer.

Set cells to always modify entered data
- Select the File tab and the Options menu before choosing the Advanced option.

- The Editing option will allow you to determine how many decimal points are shown per cell.

- The Places option determines the number of places that are shown, a positive number indicates more places, a negative number indicates fewer places. For example, if you entered a 2 into the places box, typing the number 124 would result in 1.24 being displayed.

Enter numbers in cells in sequence
- Start by adding a number to the first cell in the eventual range.

- Add the second number into the next cell in the sequence.

- Select both cells before choosing the fill handle option and dragging the handle to cover the number of cells that will encompass the sequence.

- Release the mouse and the cells should populate automatically.

Add columns and rows

- Columns and rows can be added to a worksheet by right clicking on the letter or number to the right or below of where you want the new column or row to be. New columns are always created to the left of the original and new rows are always created above the original. After adding one, more can be added by simply pressing the F4 key.

- Columns and rows can be deleted from a worksheet by right clicking on the letter or number of the column or row and selecting the delete option. Multiple columns and rows can be deleted by selecting the first and then dragging the cursor to the last. Multiple individual columns or rows can be deleted be holding down the CTRL key before clicking the delete option.

- If you wish to ensure a particular column or row is always visible, even when moving to other parts of a workbook, activate what is known as the Freezing feature. Start by selecting the column or row to the right of the column or below the row you wish to freeze. Choose the View tab and select the Freeze Pane option. You can unfreeze things the same way. This option will also let you freeze the first row or column currently visible without having to select it first.

- Columns and rows can be resized manually by clicking and dragging individual column labels as needed.

- To manually make a column or row the size of the largest cell of data in the row or column simply left click twice on the right side of the column or row header.

Formatting cells

Keep in mind that in instances where formatting of cells changes the visible value of what is displayed in the cell, the true value will be used for formula references. To access the formatting options for a cell or set of cells, select them and then right click and choose the Format Cells option.

The number tab: When you open the Format Cells option you will be greeted with the Numbers Tab which provides you with the opportunity to change how numbers in cells are displayed. You can alter how written numbers are displayed, the number of decimal places shown, how fractions are displayed, how percentages are displayed, how time and dates are displayed, how currency is displayed as well as how monetary units are displayed.

Be aware, formatting a cell for a specific type of numerical data will ensure that any other type of information entered into that cell will not be allowed or will be deleted once it has been entered. If you find you are unable to enter data into a cell, choose the format cell option and reset the cell to the default General option, you will need to reenter the data in question.

Alignment: The alignment tab under the Format Cell option is used to determine how the cell will reflect data that is entered. There are specific options to determine the orientation of text as well as its direction, indention and text wrapping options. You will also find the option to shrink text so it is completely visible in the specified cell. Finally, you will find the option to merge a group of cells so that all of the selected cells are considered a single cell. The option to unmerge cells can be found in the same place.

Font: The Font Tab contains the same options commonly found in word processing programs. You will have the option to modify the font used in the selected cell, change the style, size and color. If you are interested in adding additional effects to the data in the cells, those options are also available.

Border: The border tab provides you with the opportunity to visually differentiate individual cells with a wide variety of colors, the result will outline the selected cell or cells. The Style option will determine what the resulting border will look like, and the Color option will set the color. The remaining options are dedicated to determining which parts of the border are visible. It is important to always select the options on the left before choosing the specifics on the right.

Fill: The Fill Tab provides you with several opportunities in regards to choosing the background color of the selected cell or cells. Numerous pattern styles are also available as are additional options regarding multiple colors and shading options.

Protection: The final tab relates to protection and determines if specific cells are locked or are not visible to formulas. Individual cell options will not activate until protection for the worksheet has been turned on.

Worksheets
Working with multiple spreadsheets

- The option to switch between spreadsheets can be found at the bottom of the spreadsheet where it says Sheet 1.

- Additional sheets can be added by simply pressing the plus button next to the Sheet 1 button.

- Right clicking on Sheet 1 will bring up a list of options including renaming it, inserting new sheets (added to the left of the current worksheet) and deleting the worksheet.

- Worksheets can be repositioned in the same workbook by simply left clicking on the sheet you wish to move and dragging it to the desired location.

- Right clicking on a worksheet and selecting the move or copy option will allow you to then paste it into a different workbook. The resulting menu will allow you to choose all the specifics regarding which book it will be moved to and where in the order it will be placed.

- Right clicking on your desired worksheet will also provide you with the opportunity to lock a spreadsheet. Choose this option if you wish to close the specific worksheet to modification by others. You will be offered the opportunity to create a password when you select this option.

Editing multiple worksheets at once
- To edit multiple worksheets at once, start by selecting one of the worksheets using the tabs at the bottom of the screen.

- After selecting the first sheet, hold down the CTRL key before selecting additional sheet.

- Right clicking will then bring up all the options which are available to multiple sheets at once.

Entering data on multiple worksheets simultaneously
- Start by selecting the first worksheet you want to add the data to, followed by the desired cell.

- Click and drag to include additional cells on the same worksheet.

- Hold down the CTRL key and select the next worksheet and then click a desired cell and drag.

- Select the first cell to enter the data into and enter the data.

- Pressing the tab key should copy the data to the next cell. Continue as needed

Saving

Workbooks can be saved in a wide variety of file formats depending on several specific needs. If you find yourself in need of changing how a specific workbook is saved, start by choosing the Save As option found underneath the File tab. This will allow you to change the name of the original file so that the change doesn't affect it as well. The Save As Type option will provide you with a list of available extensions such as ODS, EXPS, PDF, XLA, XLAM, SLX, DIF, PRN, CSV, TXT, XLT, XLTM, XLTX, HTML, HTM, MHTML, MHT, XLM, XLS, XLSB, XLSM and XLSX.

Chapter 3: Sorting and Filtering Data

Sorting

Excel has a series of controls in place which will help to accurately determine when specific ranges of cells are related to one another. It requires to blank columns or rows in the related areas in order to work properly. Sorting can be done in numerous ways, text can be sorted alphabetically, numbers can be sorted highest to lowest or lowest to heist, times and dates can be sorted based on age and custom sorting includes things like cell color, font size, icon and more.

Specific sorting criteria can also be saved into individual workbooks so they are easy to reapply when the workbook is reopened. Sorting specifics can only be saved when the data included is already formatted into a table, and to format data into a table, it first needs a name.

Naming cells
- Naming this data will make it easier to refer to later, add a name in the Name Box and save it by pressing the ENTER key.

- Names cannot contain spaces and must start with a letter, a backslash or an underscore. Each name must always be unique.

- The remaining characters can be underscores, periods, numbers and letters. Excel will not distinguish capital and lowercase letters. If you wish to make the name, and therefore the cell or group of cells visible to the current workbook as a whole, add the prefix Sheet1! to the start of the name where Sheet1 is the sheet you are basing the data in.

- You can also select the group of cells you wish to name, right click and either choose a name yourself with the Define Name option or let Excel label the data for you with the Pick From Drop Down List option.

- Additional naming options can be found on the Formulas tab under the Defined Names Sections.

Naming rows and columns
- Start by selecting the row or column you wish to rename.

- View the naming options which can be found underneath the Formulas tab.

- Select the name manager option, then edit to change the name of the row or column. The scope option will determine if the change will apply to the entirety of the workbook or just the current worksheet.

Defining names
- If you have included row or columns names these can be converted into table names.

- Start by selecting the group of cells you want to be included under the name.

- Select the Formulas tab and the Defined Names grouping of options before choosing the option to Create from Selection.

- The resulting dialogue box will list any related labels that already exist and allow you to choose the one which will cover the entire table.

Creating names with the new name dialogue box
- Select the Formulas tab and the Defined Names grouping of options before choosing the Define name option.

- Add the name and the scope (workbook or worksheet) of the name. This box will also allow you the opportunity to enter a descriptive comment relating to the name which will appear when you hover your cursor over the name.

- In the box labeled Refers To, enter the cell or group of cells that the name refers to. Formulas can also be named in this fashion.

Managing named content
- Select the Formulas tab and the Defined Names grouping of options before choosing the option labeled Name Manager.

- This option will display all of the named ranges or tables that are in the current workbook. You can see names, values, what the name refers to, its scope and any related comments.

- You have the option on this screen to add new names, edit existing names and delete names.

- The button directly above the close button will highlight and show the cells the selected name refers to.

- The name manager will not appear if you are currently editing a named range or table.

Creating column and row headings
- Select the Page Layout tab before choosing the Sheet Options selection.

- From there you will be taken to the Page Setup dialogue box.

- Underneath the list of options under Print you will find the option to turn on Row and Column Headings.

Creating a table
- Start by selecting the data you wish to convert into a table.

- Select the tab labeled Insert and select the option for Tables then click the option for a single table. You can also perform this action by pressing the CTRL key in conjunction with the L key or the T key.

- If you have named individual rows and columns in relation to the range in question, make sure you select the option indicating My Table Has Headers, otherwise these will be created automatically. Ensuring headers do not show at all can be done by right clicking on the completed table, choose the Design option, the Table Style option and then deselect the Header Row option.

- Choosing the OK option will cause Excel to consider the first column as the header column and the first row and the header row for table creating purposes. To ensure proper labels appear through the worksheet, follow the steps listed in chapter 2 to free the heading columns/rows.

Formatting tables
- Data can also be formatted as a table by choosing the Home tab followed by the option for Styles and Format as Table. You will be able to choose between dark, medium and light options.

- This option will also allow you to create your own style by selecting the more option after selecting Cell Styles.

- Selecting New Table Style will allow you to name your style, before formatting using all of the formatting options available when formatting existing cells. You will have the option to preview the style you are creating as well as determining if it becomes the default when creating new tables.

- The Table Style Options grouping of options will allow you to turn headers on or off, turn totals on or off, determine if special formation is allowed and if alternating rows or columns will be alternating colors to make the table easier to read.

- If you wish to format an already existing tables simply select the table in question before following the steps listed above.

Create a dropdown list
- Start by adding content to a worksheet in contiguous cells.

- Assign a name to the data as if you were creating a table.

- Select the cell that you wish for the dropdown menu to be connected to.

- Choose the Data tab followed by the Data Validation option found in the Data Tools grouping.

- Under the Settings tab look for the box named Source and enter the name of your list preceded by the = sign.

- Under the Input Message tab enter a title and any additional message you want the dropdown list to display.

- Check the box offering In Cell Dropdown and select OK.

- You can also include a variety of error alerts to prevent incorrect data from being entered into the cell.

- When you click on the cell in question the new dropdown box should then appear.

Text
- Start by selecting the row or column of your table that you want to sort.

- The Sort And Filter group can be found on the Data tab and it will automatically allow you to sort in ascending or descending order of letters or numbers. Dates and times can also be sorted the same way.

- The Sort button will give you access to a more detailed level of sorting where you can choose the order in which multiple things are sorted. The Options button will determine if your search is case sensitive or if the sorted items are sorted top to bottom or left to right.

- If the data you are sorting is in a table then the sorting will be saved for the future. To reapply, visit the Sort group under the Data tab and select the Reapply option.

- To clear sorting in a table, select the table, visit the Sort group under the Data tab and select the clear option.

- Clicking on the header of a specific row or column header will also automatically sort that data from biggest to smallest or alphabetically.

Formatting options

- Start by selecting the row or column of your table that you want to sort.

- The Sort And Filter group can be found on the Data tab

- Select the Sort button and choose the Column option followed by Sort By.

- The resulting Sort On option will allow you to sort your table by cell color, cell icon and font color.

- Choose the order option and determine the order of the sorted items. Cells with the same color, icon or font can be all group together to the top or bottom, left or right.

- The Add Level Option will allow you to further specify ordering specifics so you can for example sort by color first, then font and finally icon.

Custom
- To create a custom sorting option, first select the File tab followed by the selection for Options.

- Choose the Advanced section and look for the Edit Custom Lists option found under the General heading.

- This option already has custom lists relating to days and months both abbreviated or non.

- Add the list you want to use to use to the box labeled List Entries and then select the add option.

- If you have already organized a table in the way you want the list to automatically copy, instead select the list in question and choose the Import option.

Filtering Data

After you have converted a range of cells into a table, you can then easily filter certain type of data out of the table automatically. Assuming you have table headers enabled (see above for more details) then each header will have an arrow at the end of its name. To filter the data

- Start by clicking the arrow of the column you want to filter.

- This will present you with a list of options including all of the variables you can deselect from the current table. This is also the list that will allow you to clear any filters that are currently applied.

- Broader filters such as numbers, text and color are also provided depending on what the current table contains.

- Additional options are available under the Data tab and the Sort and Filter grouping of Options underneath the option labeled Advanced

- Text and Number Filtering options will provide you with additional dialogue boxes that relate to the content being filtered and include custom filters that allow you to provide your own unique filters.

- Numeric filters are numbers that are equal to something specific, not equal, greater than, less than, greater than or equal to, less than or equal to, between, top 10, above average or below average

- Text filtering includes the option to filter for words that are or are not the search term, as well as those that begin or end with a certain letter and those that contain or do not contain a certain letter.

Chapter 4: All About Formulas and Functions

When it comes to spreadsheets, the words function and formula are typically used interchangeably. A formula is any expression that is used to determine the value of a specific cell or group of cells. Functions are a set of predefined formulas that are already available in Excel. When it comes to writing formulas, it is important to remember that Excel uses the order of operations when making calculations which means that any part of a calculation that can be found in parentheses is calculated first, before any other calculations come into play. When writing a formula, it is important to always start it with = so that Excel knowns to find the answer to the formula in questions

To enter functions or formulas
- Start by selecting the cell you want to contain the formula or function.

- Enter the desired function into the formula bar, making sure to start every function with an equal sign =.

- Add the formula or function you wish to use and, when done properly, the result will appear in the selected box.

- Once a cell has been given a formula, that formula can be changed in the formula box.

To switch between relative cell references and absolute cell references

Cells can be copied and pasted using common copy and paste commands. Typically, when a formula or function is added to a cell that directly references another cell or set of cells the receiving cell interprets that data in relation to itself. For example, Cell B1 sees cell A1 as one cell to the left. If you moved the data in B1 to F1, then the A1 reference would instead be seen as E1. In order to ensure your references are referring to specific cells and not directions, follow the steps below.

- Select the cell or cells you wish to change to an absolute frame of reference and press the F4 key.

- Alternatively, you can start by entering a formula into a desired cell when listing the formula make sure you include a $ before the result of the indicator of the result of the formula before ultimately pressing the Enter key.

- Select the fill handle and drag it to the desired cells, the formula will be copied using exact references.

- References can be checked by left clicking twice on any of the new cells.

To quickly enter common functions

- Start by pressing the SHIFT key in conjunction with the CTRL key and the "key. This will copy the value from the previous cell into the current cell's formula bar.

- Pressing the ' key in conjunction with just the CTRL key will show the formula working in each of your currently active cells.

- The =SUM function can be used by typing SUM(list of cells) where the list of cells is the cells you wish to add together.

Conditional Functions
AND,   OR,   NOT,   IF   written   as IF(logical_test,value_if_true,value_if_false)
- Logical_test: The condition you are looking to determine.

- Value_if_true: The value you want to appear if the condition is true.

- Value_if_false: The value that you want to appear if the condition is true.

- The function is set up in the same way for AND, OR and NOT.

Function to add and subtract units of time
- Adding periods of time together is as easy as putting the first unit of time in one cell and the other unit of time in a second cell.

- In a third cell write = the first cell + the second cell.

- Excel calculates time based on the amount elapsed from midnight. The result is displayed in full day increments

Function to determine a running balance

- Start by setting up a table that has three columns, the first column should be money going in, the second money going out and the third written as SUM(the cells in the row)

- The Sum column can then be extended using the Fill Bucket to extend the formula to include the previous sum in addition to the current sum.

Function to determine the average, mean, median and mode

- Select a cell adjacent to the group of cells you wish to find the mode, median or mean for.

- In the Home tab, find the Editing group of options and then the option labeled AutoSum, select which form of average you want to find and hit the ENTER key

- If you wish to find the Average of a group of numbers that are not next to one another, write the formula as AVERAGE, MEAN, MEDIAN, MODE(the cells in question) with the cells in question being the cells you are looking for more information on.

Function to subtract

- A subtraction function can be written as =number-number or it can be written as SUM(number, negative number) ·

- There is no specific subtraction function in Excel.

Function to multiply
- To multiply two numbers in a cell, write the function as =5*10

- To multiply a column or row by a specific number, write the formula so the cell to be constantly multiplied by is written with a pair of $ around the column designation. For example, if you wished to multiply multiple cells by cell A1 you would write it as $A$1.

- Writing the formula once and then using the Fill Bucket will allow you to multiply the entire column or row easily.

- Non-contiguous cells can be multiplied together by writing the formula as PRODUCT(cell1,cell2) where cell1 and cell2 are the cells that are being multiplied, adding a comma and an extra number inside the parentheses will multiply the cells and then the result by the extra number.

- Ranges of cells can also be multiplied by writing them as Range Cell1: Range Cell2.

Function to divide
- Writing =number1/number2 will cause the current cell to produce the results of dividing the two numbers. Not including the = in this case will cause Excel to interpret the data as a date.

- =Cell1/Cell2 will also work

- To divide a column or row by a specific number, write the formula so the cell to be constantly divided by is written with a pair of $ around the column designation. For example, if you wished to multiply multiple cells by cell A1 you would write it as $A$1.

- There is no specific function related to division

Function to raise a number to the power of x
- Writing the function as number1^number2 will result in the first number being multiplied by the power of the second number.

- POWER(cell1,cell2) will take the first cell and multiply it to the power of the second cell.

Function to find the biggest or smallest number in the range
- Assuming the numbers are all located next to one another select a cell that is connected to the other cells to receive the results before selecting the AutoSum option. The Min option will find the smallest number and the Max option will find the largest number.

- Functions to find the same when the cells in question are not located next to one another are MIN, MAX, SMALL or LARGE. These are written FUNCTION(Cell1,Cell2) including another number after the second

Cell will pull another number related to the function. For example, MAX(Cell1,Cell2,2) would find the second highest number in the set. Any number can be placed in the final number slot.

The COUNTIF function

The COUNTIF function is useful when you need to determine the exact number of times a specific word or value appears in the current worksheet.

- Writing a COUNTIF function should look like this =COUNTIF(range,criteria)

- In this case, range is the area you wish the formula to include, for example to COUNTIF columns A and B, you would write A:B.

- In this case the criteria is the data that you want Excel to search for

Function won't calculate

If you find that you have entered a specific formula into a cell that then appears to not calculate properly and instead simply lists the formula, then there are a few possible things to consider. First, double check to make sure that your cells are formatted as they should be (see Formatting Cells in chapter 2). Specifically, this problem can occur if your cell is set to Text instead of General. This frequently occurs when a new column is added next to a column that is formatted for text as it will take on the faulty formatting.

If your formatting does not seem to be the issue, it is important to ensure that you have not accidentally left the option to see all formulas on. To double check, press the CTRL key in conjunction with the ~key.

Formula won't update
If you know you have entered a function properly, but changing the references doesn't affect the results cell this is likely because of incorrect settings.

- Go to the File tab and Choose the option for Options.

- Find the option labeled Formulas on the left side of the window.

- Next, find the option for Calculation, then the check box marked Automatic and make sure it is selected.

Chapter 5: Sharing Your Work

Printing

To add page breaks to your worksheets

- Start by looking at the current page break setting by opening the Print Options dialogue box.

- To do this go to the File tab and chose the Print option. This dialogue box can also be reached by pressing the CTRL key in conjunction with the P key.

- The result should be a view of all current page breaks.

- This view can also be reached by selecting the View tab and then the Page Break Preview option.

- Choose the row or column you wish to mark the point of the break and then choose the Insert Page Break option.

- Page breaks can also be simply dragged into position by choosing the File tab, followed by Options, then Editing Options and finally Advanced.

- Check the box offering Cell Drag and Drop before selecting OK to save you choices.

- With that box checked, dragging preexisting page breaks will move them to new locations.

To preview results prior to printing

- Start by selecting the sheet or group of sheets that you want to view before printing them.

- Select the File tab before choosing the Print option and then the option to preview the sheet prior to printing.

- This option can also be selected by pressing the F2 key in conjunction with the CTRL key.

- The result options will provide you with the ability to set the margins for the printed worksheet as well as changing the footers and headers.

- This menu also provides options for repeating columns or rows in the printed version as well as adding extra gridlines, altering page or and things like showing cell errors on the printed version along with comments and any headings that are in use.

To scale the printed version

- Start by selecting the worksheet you wish to modify before selecting the Page Layout tab.

- Go to the Page Setup grouping of options and click the button next to page Setup.

- Select the Page tab and then the option related to scaling, this will allow you to make the current worksheet appear smaller or larger when printed or simply to ensure it all fits on a single page.

- The Fit To option will scale the worksheet to automatically fit on the specified number of pages. The Fit To option ignores any preexisting page breaks.

- The width as well as the height of the sheet can be set, the first box is width, the second height, and both can be set independently. Setting either to 1 will ensure the entire worksheet fits on one piece of paper.

To print only one part of a worksheet
- Go to the Page Setup grouping of options and click the button next to page Setup.

- Select the Page tab and then the option related to print area then Set Print Area.

- When you choose a selection it is important you deselect it after you have printed because it will not automatically revert to normal printing options without your input.

- If you select multiple ranges that are not close to one another, they will each print on a separate page.

Charts and Graphing

Chart basics
- Start by adding the data you will ultimately use in the chart to rows and columns in what you think will be the best fit. Excel will

automatically suggest the type of chart it thinks will best display the data. It is important that all of the data be contiguous for the Excel to understand that it is all part of the same chart.

- The data for radar charts, surface charts, area charts, line charts, bar charts and column charts can be arranged in either column form or row form and should always have headers to prevent Excel from creating them.

- Doughnut charts or pie chart data should be arranged with one row or column of labels and another of data.

- Stock chart data should be written using dates and names as labels, they should also be written as high values, then low values and finally closing values.

Column charts
Column charts are useful for data in both row or column form. Colum charts are ideal when you wish to show changes to data over time or wish to compare specific subsets of data. The average column chart places categories on the X axis and values on the Y axis.

Clustered column charts: These charts are used to determine similarities in values across multiple related categories. The standard column chart will only show values as vertical two dimensional rectangles. The 3D version of the Cluster chart simply adds depth to the two dimensional version, without actually tracking a third variable on the depth axis. Cluster column charts are ideal when you are looking to show a physical representation of disordered names, scale arrangements or broad ranges of value.

Stacked column charts: These charts show a more direct relationship between individual items in terms of the whole. They are primarily used to show how various variables contribute to a larger whole. The two dimensional version of a stacked column chart is displayed as a number of stacked 2D rectangles. The 3D version simply adds depth to the chart, it does not track a third value based on individual depth.

100 percent stacked column charts: These charts are typically used to compare how much each variable contributes to a total value but expressed in percentage points. It differs from the stacked column chart as it is more useful when there are three or more separate data series. The two dimensional version of a 100 percent column chart is displayed as a number of stacked 2D rectangles. The 3D version simply adds depth to the chart, it does not track a third value based on individual depth.

Three dimensional column chart: Unlike the other types of charts that are just dropping a two dimensional chart into a three dimensional model, a true three dimensional chart has an X, Y and Z access and all three chart a specific piece of data. Typically, categories are listed to the X and Z access while the Y axis displays variables.

Other column chart options
All the columns in column charts can also be displayed as pyramids, cones and cylinders these is purely a cosmic difference, all data will be displayed the same.

Bar charts
Bar charts are quite similar to column charts and share all the same subtypes. Bar charts are useful when it comes to illustraiting how individual items compare to one another. When it comes to choosing between the two, consider a bar chart when working with durations of time as your values or when the axis labels are longer than average.

Line charts
Line charts are a useful method of displaying data continuously over a specific amount of time. Typically, it is used to show how multiple variables performed along a set scale when compared to one another. Any data that is placed into rows or columns can be turned into a line chart and the X axis holds category data and Y axis contains the value data. Line charts are especially useful when various category labels are written as text and are spread out evenly such as quarters, months or years. If you have more than ten labels you wish to plot, a scatter chart is a better choice.

Simple line chart: Line graphs and versions of line graphs with markers to distinguish between multiple data streams are ideal when it comes to showing broad trends over a period of time, particularly when a large number of data points are being used and the order they appear in remains relevant. If you end up plotting quite a few different data streams, then you will want to avoid using markers.

Stacked line chart: Can be created to use markers or not, ideal when it comes to showing larger trends as well as the contributions of each category in relation to the whole. It is important to use markers otherwise it can be difficult to determine if the lines are actually stacked.

One hundred percent stacked line chart: Markers can be used as needed, it is useful when showing larger trends as well as how each category contributed to the end result. Stacked area charts are typically easier to discern.

Three dimensional line chart: This chart contains a third axis that can be modified based on variables. A true three dimensional chart has an X, Y and Z access and all three chart a specific piece of data. Typically, categories are listed to the X and Z access while the Y axis displays variables.

Scatter chart
Line charts and scatter charts look quite similar, even more so if you utilize the option to add lines between the scatter chart points. Despite the visual similarity, however, the two chart data along the X axis and Y axis differently. Scatter charts work differently from other charts, in that they plot values along the X axis and also values on the Y axis. These charts are useful when you need to chart two different values for a single category.

Scatter charts are also able to change the scale of the horizontal axis to deliver a greater degree of specificity. It is also useful when you want to use a horizontal axis with a logarithmic scale, when the X values are easily segmented or when there are more than 10 points on the X axis. It is also a great choice when you want to display numerous data points where time is not a factor. To prepare data for being put into a scatter chart it is important to place all of the values that you want graphed on the X axis in a single column or row and then enter the Y axis values in the next column or row.

Scatter chart with markers: This type of scatter chart will compare a set of values and is best used when the addition of lines between the points would only lead to confusion of if the individual points are not expressly related.

Scatter chart with lines: The points on a scatter chart can be expressed with a line as well as markers or without. A line with no markers is typically useful when expressing an overall trend without a regard for specifics.

Pie chart
For data that can be expressed in a single column or row, the best choice to display it visually is typically a pie chart. Pie charts are typically used to show individual parts of whole in relation to the combined total of all of the parts in question. The percentage of each categories contribution will also be displayed as a percentage. Pie charts are the perfect choice when none of the relative values are negative, none of the values are zero, there are no more than seven categories being graphed and, most importantly, all of the values are related to a larger whole.

Standard pie chart: The most common variation of the pie chart can be displayed in either two or three dimensions, though the added dimension does not map to any variables and is just for show. Each section of the pie chart can also be left clicked on for additional emphasis.

Pie of pie chart: This pie chart will display the specific breakdown of one of the sections with its own pie chart or bar graph. This is the right type of chart to use if one section of the pie chart is too complex to simply be reduced to a single slice.

Exploded pie chart: This version of the standard pie chart gives each individual section add emphasis by placing space between each. This version of the pie chart can also be shown in two or three dimensions though the added dimension does not map to any variables and is just for show.

Doughnut charts
Doughnut charts are similar to pie charts in that they show individual values related to specific categories in terms of percentage of a larger whole. Doughnut charts are used instead of pie charts when more than one value is being tracked per category. In many situations a stacked bar graph is easier to read than a doughnut graph. Doughnut charts contain all the various subtypes as pie charts

Area charts
Area charts are useful for making the magnitude of a category's values change over time more readily visible. They are also an easy way to emphasize each value in relation to the whole. Area charts

typically show a variety of plotted values as well as their sum total.

Standard area chart: A standard area chart can be displayed in two or three dimensions, the unstacked variation of this 2D version can be difficult to view as parts of the data will be obscured. The 3D version allows you to include a third variable for the Z axis to chart though it can still be difficult to see all the layers of data.

Stacked area chart: This version of the area chart is the most commonly used as it displays various categories on top of one another for easy comparison. This version of the area chart can also be shown in two or three dimensions though the added dimension does not map to any variables and is just for show.

One hundred percent stacked area chart: These charts are typically used to compare how much each variable contributes to a total value but are expressed in percentage points. It differs from the stacked area chart as it more useful when there are three or more separate data series. The two dimensional version of a one hundred percent column chart are displayed as a number of stacked 2D rectangles. The 3D version simply adds depth to the chart, it does not track a third value based on individual depth.

Creating a simple chart
- Start by selecting all of the data that you want to include in the chart. You may also select a single cell and Excel will determine what other cells contain related data.

Instead of clicking and dragging you may also select the first cell, hold down the SHIFT key and then select the last cell.

- Chart options are available from the Insert tab in the charts grouping.

- Each various type of chart has its own list of options which can be found by clicking the arrow beneath its picture. Created charts are embedded in their current worksheet by default

Changing a chart's location
- Once a chart has been embedded, you can move it to a different location in another worksheet or workbook by first selecting it by left clicking on it.

- The resulting Chart Tools option will now have new tabs for Format, Layout and Design.

- Select the Design tab and look for the Move Chart option in the Location grouping of options.

- The option to determine where to move the chart will be displayed and you will be able to choose the option to add the chart to a new sheet or other existing workbooks or worksheets.

- In order to make the chart embed properly in the new sheet it is important to select the Object In box and make sure it includes the destination worksheet.

Change the style of a chart or the way it is laid out automatically

Charts that have already been created can also be changed on the fly through the use of numerous predefined options. These predefined options can be further defined based on specific needs and preferences.

- Start by selecting the chart that you wish to change which will bring up the Chart Tools options list while at the same time ensuring the Format, Layout and Design tabs are readily accessible.

- The Design Tab will provide access to the Chart Layout grouping of options which will allow you to modify some basic visual elements of your current chart.

- Alternatively, you can use the Chart Styles grouping of options to modify your chart in a variety of ways primarily related to presentation color. Additional varieties will be available by clicking on the More arrow.

Change the style of a chart or the way it is laid out manually

- Individual elements of each chart can also be changed manually, to do so start by selecting the chart that you want to edit to bring up the Chart Tools menu with Format, Layout and Design enabled.

- Select the Format tab and then the Current Selection grouping where the arrow to the right of the Chart Elements option will provide you with access to a variety of chart elements.

- Options will include shape styles, shape effects, shape outline, shape fill.

- Text can be altered with a variety of effects as well as individual filling and outlining options. If you add anything using WordArt it cannot be removed later, it can only be changed or deleted.

- The Layout Tab will provide you with access to various elements as well including labels, data presentation, the legend for the chart, the labels on each axis, visibility of gridlines and the label for the chart. If 3D chart variations are enabled, then 3D options will also be available here.

Add/remove chart titles

Adding titles to charts and individual chart X and Y axes provides an easy way to make complex information more readily apparent. Title options can be found under Chart Tools once a chart has been selected to allow the access to the Format, Layout and Design tabs.

- To add a title to a chart select the Layout tab and the grouping of options titled Labels to find the Chart Title option.

- A box will appear labeled Box Title, fill it in and determine where you want the title to be placed.

- Text formation options will appear once the text is highlighted; traditional formatting options will also be available.

- To add titles to the axes, start by selecting the preferred chart and then viewing the Layout tab, the Labels grouping of options and the option labeled Axis titles.

- This option will provide you with the opportunity to label all the axes including multiple X or Y axes. To add a title for the Z axis, select the option labeled Depth Axis Title.

- Enter a title and you will be provided with formatting options as well.

Adding data point labels

Individual labels can be added to specific data point in some charts to emphasis specific areas of importance.

- To add a single label to all data points in a specific series or to a single point in a series start by selecting the desired chart to pull up the Chart Tools option.

- Select the layout tab, followed by the Labels grouping of options and the option for Data Labels

- This will provide you with options when it comes to naming individual or multiple labels as well as removing unneeded labels as well.

Add a legend

A legend is a quick and easy way to ensure that everyone viewing your chart knows exactly what they are looking at.

- To add a legend to a specific chart start by selecting the desired chart to pull up the Chart Tools option.

- Select the Layout tab and the grouping of options titled Labels to find the Legend option.

- Select the options related to your specific graph, additional options are available under the More Legend Options button.

- Legend adjustments can be made through this window or by dragging the legend using the mouse. Adjustments made through the options menu will automatically populate and make adjustments to data placing as needed.

- Selecting the legend and hitting the delete key will remove the legend from the chart.

- Selecting the individual legend entries will allow you to edit them individually.

Modify chart size

- Charts can be moved or resized by simply dragging them as required.

- Charts can also be resized from the Format tab by selecting the Size grouping of options then Shape Width and Shape Height. Entering a number and pressing the ENTER key will automatically make the requested changes.

- Additional options are located in the same place on the ribbon under the button next to the Size label. Here you will be able to determine if you want the chart to scale, rotate or be resized.

- The properties tab provides controls regarding how the chart moves in relation to how cells more or are resized in the worksheet.

Create a chart template
If you personalize a chart in such a way that you will want to use it again, that chart can be saved as a template for future use.
- Start by selecting the chart that you will want to save for future use.

- Select the Design tab and look for the grouping of options labeled Type and choose the Save as Template option.

- By default, after you enter a name for the template, it will be viewable under the Templates option in the Insert Chart menu.

- Giving the template a name and saving it will populate future charts with all of the colors, format and height and width specifications as the original. It can then be modified as normal.

- The template will be available across worksheets and workbooks.

Chapter 6: Error Messages and Bonus Tips

Common Error Messages

If you enter a function or formula into a cell and the result is an error message, then it is likely you didn't quite get everything right the first time. The error message that appears is not random, however, and what is displayed in the cell will give you an idea of what you need to fix to get the answer you were looking for.

- *#NULL!* Will appear if you list a point where two ranges intersect and they do not actually intersect at that point.

- *#DIV/o!* Will appear if your formula attempts to divide by zero.

- *#Value!* Will appear if one of the variables in your formula is an incorrect type based on Excel's specifications. This typically occurs if a text value is in the wrong place.

- *#REF!* Will appear if the formula you have entered references a cell that does not contain information.

- *#NAME?* Will appear if the formula has an unrecognized name or if some of the text within the formula returns as unrecognized.

- *#NUM!* Will appear if the formula contains a number that is somehow invalid.

- *#N/A* Will appear if a certain value that is referenced cannot be used by a specific formula.

If a cell returns ####

This issue can occur for several reasons, the simplest being that the cell in question is not large enough to show the entire result. Resizing the cell should be your first recourse. If the cell continues to show #### regardless of its width, then the next most likely scenario is that the cell is trying to display a time or date but the given information does not fit into the required structure. Double check what is meant to be in the cell and any formulas or formatting that is on the cell, just in case. Also double check to ensure the cell has the appropriate formatting (see Formatting Cells in chapter 2).

Tips
Remove duplicates
Removing duplicate information automatically in larger worksheets can be a significant timesaver and can make convoluted sheets much easier to sift through.

- Start by selecting the data you want to remove the duplicates from.

- Visit the Data tab and under the Tools grouping you will find the option to remove duplicates. This will remove individual cells with duplicated data as well as entire rows or columns.

Turn rows into columns
- Begin by highlighting the row or column you wish to change into a column or row.

- Right click on your selection and chose the option for Paste Special

- Select the transpose option from the resulting dialogue box and select OK to confirm your selection.

Split a cell into multiple cells
- Start by selecting the data you wish to manipulate

- Visit the Data tab and select the option labeled Text to Columns under the Data Tools grouping.

- The resulting options will provide you with several choices including Delimited which will allow you to break up the cells information based on tabs, spaces or commas. Delimited options include custom options so you can use any character you choose.

- The Fixed Width option will allow you to choose exactly where the split will occur.

Try conditional formatting
Conditional formatting will allow you to change things such as the color or font used in the cell based on information with the cell.
- Conditional formatting options can be found on the Home tab under the Styles grouping.

- When you first select it you will notice a wide variety options when it comes to what conditional formatting can do. Start by choosing New Formatting Rule.

- From this new screen you can choose the type of rule that you can result in the formatting. Consider minimum and maximum values as well as color gradients for each.

- Rule types include formatting all cells based on their values, formatting only cells that contain specific values, formatting only the highest and lowest ranked values, formatting only values that are above or below the average, formatting only values that are unique, formatting only the values that are the same and use a formula to determine cell formatting.

Adding an Excel chart to a word document
- Start by selecting the chart you wish to move into a word document.

- Press the CTRL key in conjunction with the C key to copy the chart to the clipboard.

- In the Word document, choose where you want the chart to be, this can be tricky as word documents are limited when it comes to spacing concerns.

- On the Edit menu, look for the Paste Special option.

- This will open a new dialogue box, choose the option for an Excel Worksheet Object

- Select the paste link option on the left side of the dialogue box.

- This will allow you to then view the chart in Microsoft Word, but you will not be able to edit any part of the chart further, make sure it is right before you copy it.

Conclusion Excel for Everyone

Thank you again for purchasing this book! I hope it was able to help provide you with everything you need in order make the most out of the spreadsheet program that has most likely been on your computer for years. Excel can do almost anything you can possibly imagine; you just need to know how to set it in motion. While it may seem difficult at first, with practice everything that initially takes hour will someday be finished in what just seems like seconds.

The next step is to stop reading already and start practicing. Remember, using Excel properly is a skill, and like any other skill it needs to be used regularly if you ever hope to improve.

Finally, if you enjoyed this book, then I'd like to ask you for a favor, would you be kind enough to leave a review for this book on Amazon? It'd be greatly appreciated!

Excel:

Strategic Use of the Calc Spreadsheet in Business Environments

Data Analysis and Business Modeling

Author
Francesco Iannello

The following information is presented purely for informative purposes and is therefore considered universal. The information presented within is done so without a contract or any other type of assurance as to its quality or validity.

Any trademarks which are used are done so without consent and any use of the same does not imply consent or permission was gained from the owner. Any trademarks or brands found within are purely used for clarification purposes and no owners are in anyway affiliated with this work.

Introduction Excel for Business

I want to thank you and congratulate you for purchasing *Excel: Strategic Use of the Calc Spreadsheet in Business Environments, Data Analysis and Business Modeling.* Spreadsheets are a fact of modern life and with this book you have taken the first step to learning to create them to ensure maximum effectiveness and efficiency. You will be surprised at all the things you can do when given a little knowledge, and a little more practice. Get ready to get to it and you will soon be creating spreadsheets better than anyone in your office.

This book contains proven steps and strategies designed to ensure you can make the most of data validation, functions regarding matrices, as well as conditional formulas. Tips are given to make the most of the various types of lookup and filter features available including the best use of defined names, VLOOKUP, HLOOKUIP and additional advanced filters. You will also find a detailed explanation of how to activate the developer tab and then use it to create timesaving macros without having to learn a programing language. Finally, there is a discussion of Pivot tables, Power Pivot and Power View and how the three work together for maximum efficiency.

Thanks again for purchasing this book, I hope you enjoy it!

Chapter 1: Data Validation Functioning

Data validation is a spreadsheet feature which can provide you with the ability to create a list of specific entries which will then restrict what values you can place in each cell. You can also create a message elaborating on what types of data will be allowed in the cells, add warnings when the wrong type of data is put into a cell and check for cells filled with the wrong information through the use of the Audit function. Finally, you can set a range of specific values to be placed in any cell or determine this range based on the results of a different cell.

Allow a set of entries to be entered into a cell
To ensure a specific set of values are the only values that a specific cell or set of cells will accept, you must first create an acceptable list of values before setting the cell to only accept those values. The steps for doing so are outlined below:

1. Begin by clicking on cell A1 to select it

2. Go to the menu labeled Data before choosing the option for Validation

3. Select the option for settings, then choose the List option from the drop-down menu.

4. Find the box labeled Source, and fill it in with a,b,c before confirming your selection. This box can also be filled with a range which has been named or a specific reference to a cell which contains a set of values listed. If you chose one of these options, enter = before entering the specifics.

5. When done correctly, A1 will now show a list which provides all the acceptable values. What you select will then appear in the cell. Values can also be typed into the cell though only allowed numbers will remain in the cell.

Add a message listing allowed data
After creating a message, it will appear every time you select the cell which it is attached to. This message can be moved to a new location or, if Office Assistant is active, the message will appear there instead.

1. Choose the cell you wish to add the message to.

2. Select the menu labeled Data before selecting the option labeled Validation and choosing the tab labeled Input Message.

3. Ensure the box indicating the message will be shown is checked

4. Select the box labeled Title before typing a title for your message before selecting the message box and entering in your message. Ensure you click OK or nothing will be saved.

Add a message to show when the wrong data has been entered
These messages come in two types, those which prevent the wrong type of data be added to the cell or range of cells in question and those which don't. Limits can also be set on what can be entered into the cells without any message displaying.

1. Choose the cell you wish to add the message to.

2. Select the menu labeled Data before selecting the option labeled Validation and choosing the tab labeled Error Alert.

3. Ensure the show alert box is checked before determining the type of message you want to set.

4. If you want to create the type of message that won't allow the wrong values to be added to a cell choose the list labeled Style and select the Stop option. Add a title for the message in the box labeled Title and the bulk of the message in the box labeled Message. The message should list what values are allowed. Ensure you click OK or nothing will be saved.

5. If you want to create a message that will warn the user of incorrect values, instead visit the Style list and choose the Warning option. This will force the user to choose to continue when incorrect values are added to specific cells. Add a title for the message in the box labeled Title and the bulk of the message in the box labeled Message. The message should list what values are allowed. Ensure you click OK or nothing will be saved.

6. If you want to create a message that will simply inform the user to incorrect values, instead visit the Style list and choose the Inform option. Add a title for the message in the box labeled Title and the bulk of the message in the box labeled Message. The message should list what values are allowed.

Ensure you click OK or nothing will be saved.

Use the Audit toolbar to find improper entries
After you have set limits as to what data can be applied to which cells, this technique will allow you double check that all of the information has been entered using acceptable values. Incorrect cells will be circled for easy identification.

1. Select the menu labeled tools before choosing the option labeled Customize.

2. Chose the option labeled Toolbars from the resulting dialog window before ensuring the box labeled Auditing is already selected and closing the window.

3. Select the toolbar labeled Auditing before choosing the option related to circling data which is invalid.

4. Fixing the errors will remove the circle.

Choose the range of values a cell will allow
Different minimums and maximums can be set for each cell. This process will also allow you to see if the cell you are working on will then affect other cells based on your current actions.

1. Choose the cell you wish to add minimums or maximums to.

2. Select the menu labeled Data before selecting the option labeled Validation and choosing the tab labeled Settings.

3. Select the list labeled Allow and choose the option for whole numbers.

4. Choose the option labeled Data and then select Between.

5. Enter a minimum and a maximum number or a set of reference cells depending on your needs and click on OK to ensure your specifics are saved.

Validate a cell based on the contents of another cell
Cells can also be set to only allow certain values based on their relationship to other cells.

1. Select the menu labeled Data before selecting the option labeled Validation and choosing the tab labeled Settings.

2. Choose the list labeled Allow and the option labeled Customize.

3. Select the formula box and add the following to it: =IF(cell1>cell2, TRUE,FALSE) where cell1 and cell2 are the cells you wish to relate to one another. This formula can be used with any function, not just IF, it must always contain the equal sign as well as the true and false evaluation.

4. Select OK to save your function.

Chapter 2: Conditional Formulas

Your spreadsheet program most likely has a number of conditional rules when it comes to formatting. If what is available doesn't seem to be adequate to meet your needs, you can instead use formulas to keep things exactly how you like them. Conditional formulas can use OR, AND or IF types of logic to create formulas that only apply at certain times.

The steps listed below have replaced what in earlier versions of the spreadsheet program was known as the Conditional Sum Wizard. This add-on is no longer available, though the formulas that it created will still work when they are placed into the formula bar. They can also be added to specific cells by selecting a cell, then choosing the Formulas option, the option to Add a Function and then pasting the formula in the box labeled Function Arguments.

Use conditional formulas for formatting or data finding purposes
1. Choose the cell or group of cells that you wish to apply formatting to.

2. Select the tab labeled Home, then the tab for Conditional Formatting and finally the option to create a New Rule.

3. Selecting the option that will allow you to choose which cells will be formatted.

4. Select the box to insert values for the format based on the formula and enter the formula of your choice (copy and pasting is easiest)

5. Select the option for Formating before choosing things like fill, border, font and more to determine the specifics you will be changing based on your formula.

6. Choose OK to accept your choices, they will then be displayed based on your formula.

Conditional formula examples
- To point out cells which are currently blank: select the cells you want to check, follow the steps above and then enter this formula =Cell1="" where Cell1 is the first cell you wish to check.

- To point out cells which contain the same values: follow the steps above and then enter this formula =COUNTIF($A$1:$D$11,D2)>1

- To find the average of a set of cells: start by choosing which cell will contain the answer before entering this formula =Cell1>AVERAGE(Cell1:Cell2) where Cell1 is the first cell in the list and Cell2 is the last cell in the list.

- To find all of the values that meet multiple specific conditions enter =AND (the specifics you are looking for). Cells which meet the conditions will say true, the rest will read false.

- To find a list of values that meet one of a variety of conditions enter =OR(the specifics you are looking for). Cells which meet at least one of the conditions will say true, the rest will read false.

- To change what phrase the cells list into something besides true and false enter =IF(AND(your specifications), "Phrase1,"Phrase2") where phrase 1 and phrase 2 are what you wish to replace true and false with.

- To add a variety of tiered grades based on values in certain cells, selected the cells you wish to grade then enter =IF(cell1>number1,"grade1" IF(cell1>number2,"grade2" etc. In this case cell1 is the first cell in the list, number 1 is the first tier of grading and grade 1 is what will be displayed as a result.

Copying conditional formulas and formatting
- To copy a conditional formula or format to additional data or to an additional worksheet, start by selecting the cell whose formatting and formula you wish to copy

- Next, select the Format Painter Option found underneath the Home tab. Your pointer should then become a paint brush.

- Drag the paintbrush to the group of cells you wish to apply the formula and the formatting to. The formatting will transfer intact and the specific references of the formula will have to be modified manually to reflect the new set of cells.

- To determine how the references, you are using are interpreted by the spreadsheet start by selecting the cell which houses the formula.

- Choose which reference you want to change then press the F4 key to determine how the reference is read by the spreadsheet.

- Cell references are set to relative by default which means that each cell reads the reference in relation to its current location.

- Absolute references mean that when a reference lists cell A1 that cell is used as part of the formula regardless of where the formula is applied

- The paintbrush can be deselected with the ESC key and can be summoned again with its current specifications by clicking twice on the Format Painter option.

To remove conditional formulas and formatting
- To remove a conditional formula or format from a set of cells or an entire worksheet, start by selecting the cells whose formatting and related formulas you wish to remove.

- Select the tab labeled Home before choosing the option for Conditional Formatting.

- Choose the option labeled Data Validation followed by the box marked Same.

- Now select the option to clear rules and the option to clear the rules from the cells you selected.

- To clear all of the worksheet's formatting, select the Clear Rules option from the Conditional Formatting tab and finally choose the option to remove formatting from the full worksheet if that is what you wish to do.

Chapter 3: Matrixal Functions

Matrices can be calculated using spreadsheets in a number of ways, the MMULT function is used to determine the result of multiplying two arrays which are used as stand-ins for matrices, the MUNIT function is used to determine the matrix of a unit when given a specific dimensional reference, the MDETERM function is used to determine the measure of scale for a square matrix and the MINVERSE function is used to determine the inverse of a matrix square.

MMULT function
The correct format for this type of function is MMULT(array1, array2) where each array is a series of values spread throughout a number of cells which, when taken as a whole, represent a pair of matrices. Each array should be written as Cell1:Cell2 where Cell1 is the first cell of the matrix and Cell2 is the second. These arrays can also be written as references or constants. Array formulas are not available if you are using the program known as Excel Online.

To produce an array result for this function after you enter it into the function bar make sure you press the CTRL key, the SHIFT key and the ENTER key at the same time. You will know you entered the function correctly if the function is then surrounded by a pair of {}. Placing them manually will not work, the spreadsheet must add them using the process outlined above.

The result will contain the number of rows that matrix 1 does while containing the number of columns that matrix 2 has. To determine the correct matrix product, you must ensure that the first matrix contains the same number of columns as the second matrix has rows. The result will be displayed in an area of the worksheet that you have previously selected. It is important to select the number of cells equal to what the result will be or else the spreadsheet will only show the numbers from the resulting matrix that you selected.

Common MMULT error messages include #VALUE! which occurs when any of the cells listed in the array don't contain numerical values or are completely empty. It will also appear if the columns and rows don't line up properly. The message #N/A will occur in all of the cells that are not part of the result.

MUNIT function
The correct format for this function is MUNIT(dimension). In this case, dimension represents a value that determines the precise dimension of the matrix in question. This number will always be above zero. To produce an array result for this function after you enter it into the function bar make sure you press the CTRL key, the SHIFT key and the ENTER key at the same time. You will know you entered the function correctly if the function is then surrounded by a pair of {}. Placing them manually will not work, the spreadsheet must add them. You must have selected a number of cells to be filled with the array information for this function to work properly. The error #VALUE! will be presented if the dimension number in the function is empty, 0 or text instead of a number. The rest of the cells will be tagged as

#N/A. It is important to select the number of cells equal to what the result will be or else the spreadsheet will only show up the numbers from the resulting matrix that you selected.

MDETERM function

The proper format for this function is MDETERM(array) and in this case the array can be written as Cell1:Cell2 where Cell1 is the first cell in a square matrix and Cell2 is the final cell in the matrix. Don't forget, square matrices have an equal number of columns and rows. The array can be written as either a range of specific cells, a list of the numbers included in the array or the name of either of these if the array in question has a specific name.

To produce an array result for this function after you enter it into the function bar make sure you press the CTRL key, the SHIFT key and the ENTER key at the same time. You will know you entered the function correctly if the function is then surrounded by a pair of {}. Placing them manually will not work, the spreadsheet must add them. You must have selected a number of cells to be filled with the array information for this function to work properly. It is important to select the number of cells equal to what the result will be or else the spreadsheet will only show up the numbers from the resulting matrix that you selected.

The determinant matrix that is spit out as a result of this function is computed based on the values present in the array. Assuming this is a 3/3 square matrix this can be written as A1((B2)(C3) − (B3)(C2))+A2((B3)(C2)+A2((B3)(C1) − (B1)(C3) +

A3((B1)(C2) − (B2)(C1). The determinant of the matrix is most commonly used for finding the answer to complicated mathematical problem with multiple variables. MDETERM is useful for finding answers to the sixteenth digit which can lead to errors with larger matrices.

MINVERSE function
The formula for this function is MINVERSE(array) and in this case the array can be written as Cell1:Cell2 where Cell1 is the first cell in a square matrix and Cell2 is the final cell in the matrix. The result will have the same number of columns and rows as the original square matrix. You will always be able to multiply a matrix with its inverse to create the identity matrix. Matrices without inverses are known as singular matrices.

To produce an array result for this function after you enter it into the function bar make sure you press the CTRL key, the SHIFT key and the ENTER key at the same time. You will know you entered the function correctly if the function is then surrounded by a pair of {}. Placing them manually will not work, the spreadsheet must add them. You must have selected a number of cells to be filled with the array information for this function to work properly. It is important to select the number of cells equal to what the result will be or else the spreadsheet will only show up the numbers from the resulting matrix that you selected.

Chapter 4: Vertical Lookup/Horizontal Lookup

Vertical Lookup (VLOOKUP) and Horizontal Lookup (HLOOKUP) are two of the spreadsheet program's reference and lookup functions which are useful for finding a specific bit of data or range of data in a specific row or column.

VLOOKUP
In order to make full use of VLOOKUP, it is important to arrange information so that the data you are looking for is always located to the right of the information you will use to find the information you need. VLOOKUP searches columns for related information.

The VLOOKUP function is written as follows VLOOKUP(lookup_value, table_array, col_index_num, [range_lookup].
- In this instance the lookup_value is the value you have which relates to the value you are looking for.
- The table_array represents the cells that will be searched written as Cell1:Cell2 with Cell1 representing the first cell to be searched and Cell2 representing the final cell to be searched.
- The col_index_num is the column number that will contain the information that you are looking for.
- Finally, range_lookup can be written as either TRUE or FALSE. If you select true, the VLOOKUP will find the closest possible match given your parameters. If you select

false, then the VLOOKUP will only return exact matches.

HLOOKUP
Like VLOOKUP, HLOOKUP is useful for searching information when you have one value and you are looking for another. If you plan on using HLOOKUP it is important to arrange information so that the data you are looking for is always located beneath of the information you will use to find the information you need.

The HLOOKUP function is written as follows HLOOKUP(lookup_value, table_array, col_index_num, [range_lookup].

- In this instance the lookup_value is the value you have which relates to the value you are looking for.
- The table_array represents the cells that will be searched written as Cell1:Cell2 with Cell1 representing the first cell to be searched and Cell2 representing the final cell to be searched.
- The col_index_num is the column number that will contain the information that you are looking for.
- Finally, range_lookup can be written as either TRUE or FALSE. If you select true, the HLOOKUP will find the closest possible match given your parameters. If you select false, then the HLOOKUP will only return exact matches.

Possible Problems

- If you get the wrong result, make sure you are sorting your initial column or row either numerically or alphabetically depending on the list. If you can't sort the column in that way, ensure that your range_lookup is set to false.

- If you get a result saying #N/A then either your lookup_value is written incorrectly and is currently too small for your table_array or, if you range_lookup has been set to false, then the result you are looking for is not available.

- If you get a result saying #REF! in cell, then it is likely that your col_index_num is larger than the total number of columns currently listed in your table_array.

- If you get a result saying #VALUE! in cell then it is time to check your table array as it is likely set to a number that is smaller than 1, it may also be blank.

- If you get a result saying #NAME? in cell, it is likely because you did not include quotes around a word. If you are searching for information on a person or thing based on its, make sure there is a quotation mark on either side of it.

Ease of use
- Ensure all of the references you use for range_lookup are absolute. Cell references are set to relative by default which means that each cell reads the reference in relation

to its current location. To set them to absolute, choose which reference you want to change then press the F4 key to determine how the reference is read by the spreadsheet.

- Write dates using numbers, not letters. Writing them as words will cause issues when they are written in the first column and are used as data for table_array. To change a text date to a numerical date simply use the DATEVALUE function by typing the following =DATEVALUE(Cell1) and pressing the ENTER key. In this instance Cell1 is the cell whose date you wish to change. This will turn the date into the serial number for that day which is how many days that day is removed from the first day of January in the year 1900 (serial number 1)

- Make use of the asterisk and the question mark in the lookup_value section. A question mark will register as a match with any character in the same location as it and an asterisk is used to represent any number of characters. To look up information that contains either of these characters, place a ~ in front of them.

- Take care not to include things like extra spaces either before or after the data, any type of quotation marks or any characters that will not print in your first column. These will all cause both VLOOKUP and HLOOKUP to return faulty results.

- The clean function can be used to delete any characters in your worksheet that cannot be printed. It is best to use it on the first column of any worksheet you are planning to use VLOOKUP or HLOOKUP on just in case. The syntax for this function is CLEAN(Cell1:Cell2) with Cell1 representing the first cell to be searched and Cell2 representing the final cell to be searched.

- The trim function is used to remove all unnecessary spaces from a cell or group of cells. It removes any space that is not directly separating two characters. The syntax for this function is Trim(Cell1:Cell2) with Cell1 representing the first cell to be searched and Cell2 representing the final cell to be searched.

Chapter 5: Management of the Name Box

The spreadsheet program allows you to easily name cells or groups of cells for quick reference later on. Defined names can also be added to specific values or formulas so that any user will always know what certain parts of any workbook pertains to. A range of cells does not have to be contiguous in order to be given a defined name. After it has been defined, the name can then be used in additional cells or ranges as a type of shorthand. Names can overlap on specific cells, in these cases both names will be displayed when that cell is selected.

While on the surface, naming ranges of cells might not seem that useful, once you have gotten used to using them regularly however, you will never want to go back.
Reasons to try defined names include:

- Ranges with names are easier to remember and provide context which makes it easier to come back to when working on the same workbook in spurts for months or years at a time.

- Ranges with names are saved automatically for easy navigation. To view your current named items, use the Edit tab followed by Goto and then select the Name box. The find function can also be used to find any range with a name in the current workbook.

- Ranges with names can also be easily changed which then automatically updates all references when it comes to validation scenarios, conditional formatting scenarios, in charts and in pivot tables. In short, in any scenario where accessing specific references can otherwise easily become complicated and time consuming.

- Ranges with names are easier to remove from references or otherwise edit than regular ranges. Ranges with names are saved in such a way that they can be edited, removed or replaced without having to manually fix each reference to the range in question.

Rules for names
The naming conventions for defined names are rather specific:
- The first character of the name must be either a letter, a backslash or an underscore. The letters characters C, c, R and r cannot be used for names as they are all used as shorthand for columns and rows. The remaining characters of the name can be made up of any of the above as well as periods or numbers.

- Defined names can't be direct cell references.

- Defined names can be up to 255 individual characters, spaces are not allowed.

- Names are not case specific.

Defined name scope

A specific defined name can either be tied to a single worksheet or to an entire workbook. The scope of a particular defined name can be seen based on how the name is written, which is also how the spreadsheet program will know to find it if you have a different worksheet open while searching for it.

- Simple names like Example_01 are automatically considered to be worksheet exclusive.

- To make a defined name apply to the entirety of the current workbook, an additional prefeix is needed. Sheet#!Example_01 is how the name should be written where sheet# is equal to the current worksheet number. The Worksheet number and the defined name must be separated with an exclamation point.

Creating a range with a name using the name box
Creating individual ranges with names can be accomplished in several ways. The first involves using the Name box which can be found next to the Formula box.

- Start by chose the cell or rage you with to name before selecting the name box and typing in the new name of the cell or range of cells. Press the ENTER key to confirm your change.

- The name will not be saved if it contains invalid information.

The name box is easy to use, but it does have a number of drawbacks including the fact that you cannot use it to create duplicate names even if they are found in different worksheets. In addition, names cannot be edited using the name box and the name box will not show the full scope of a range with a name. Finally, the name box is only good for creating defined names on the currently selected worksheet.

Name Manager
The Name Manger set of options can be found under the formula tab. To create a new name:

- Begin by selecting the cell or range of cells that you wish to name.

- Choose the option to Define Name from the Name Manager options.

- The resulting box will let you set the name of the range or cell in question as well as the scope of the name.

- After confirming your selection, you can edit it by selecting the Refers To option and choosing a new range or editing what you previously typed.

- The dialogue box for the Name Manager window can easily be extended by dragging on it until you can see all of the information you need on a specific defined name.

Creating defined names automatically
Defined names can also be created automatically based on the names given to columns as well as rows. This can be done by selecting the option to Create Names from Selection in the Name Manager

set of options found on the Formulas tab. If you plan on using this method of creating names, then it is important to start using it as soon as you start the new workbook and stick with it as things can get confusing otherwise. Keep the following in mind when using this option:

- Label your rows and columns so you will recognize them when defined names are added. Spaces will be replaced with underscores.

- Defined names will only refer to cells which contain data, not the column or row labels.

- All the defined names created in this way will be workbook specific.

Chapter 6: Filters

There are a number of filters that can be applied to worksheets or parts of worksheets that will make it much easier to find the data you are looking for as quickly as possible. Filters can be set to sort by numerical values, dates or text. Multiple filters can be applied to sort results even further. Your columns should have header rows for maximum sorting efficacy. Your data will also need to be in the form of a table for the filter options to take effect. For optimum results, it is best not to mix data types such as words and numbers in the same column as only one of the character types can be filtered at a time.

Add a filter
- Choose the filter from the group labeled Filter and Sort which can be found under the Data tab.

- This will cause an arrow to appear in each column header, clicking on this arrow will provide filtering options for each column.

- You will be presented with options to determine which data you can see as well as which data you can hide.

- Columns can be sorted alphabetically, reverse alphabetically, by color, by type or by any other qualifiers you may have added.

Add a second filter
- Add the first filter as normal

- Choose the filtered column and select the filter option to add a second filter. Approving the second filter will automatically apply it on top of the first

- Filters can be cleared from the same menu using the option labeled clear filter. You will be given the option to clear one or more of the current filters. Clicking the filter option from the tab labeled data can also be used to quickly turn filtering on or off.

Searching as a type of quick filtering
If you know you are only looking for a specific type cell or set of cells with a very specific type of data, then you can use the search command to filter everything else out.

- Choose the Filter option under the tab labeled Data.

- Choose the arrow in the column you wish to filter.

- Choose the search option and enter the search data. This data can be further broken down in ways that are listed below the search box. Confirm your results and the column will be filtered.

Advanced Filters
More advanced filters can be used to filter out cells based on the number of characters they contain or even words they don't contain. This can also be accessed from the drop down arrows that appear at the top of named columns after selecting the Filter option from the tab labeled Data. Advanced options

can be found by selecting the Text Filter option. Here you will be given the option to add one or more of the advanced filters. You can enter specific text or select from dropdown menus.

Date filters are also available from the same dropdown menu. Your spreadsheet will automatically know the current date and time and let you filter information from both the past and the future. If your data is number heavy, a variety of number filters are also available, you will be able to filter out specific numbers, values that are equal to, not equal to, greater than, less than, between, above or below a specific average, in the top 10 or anything custom you can think of.

When creating filters, a question mark will register as a match with any character in the same location as it and an asterisk is used to represent any number of characters. To look up information that contains either of these characters, place a ~ in front of them.

Filters won't refresh automatically every time you open a specific workbook, to update the filters you simply need to reapply them by first selecting the columns in need of a refresh, going to the Filter and Sort tab and choosing the reapply option. A macro can also be created to automatically reapply all filters whenever the workbook is opened.

Use a slicer to filter data
Slicers are a type of visual filter that was added to spreadsheet programs in 2010 as a way to differentiate pivot tables. Assuming you are running a current version of the software, this type

of filter can now be added to other types of tables as well. Slicers can be added to any table by simply selecting that table, choosing the Insert tab and selecting the option to insert a slicer. The slicers option can also be found on the Design tab and the TABLE Tools tab.

Selecting the slicer option will provide you with several choices depending on the data you have available. Selecting your desired option will create a slider in the workbook that you can then manipulate in order to visualize specific data. You are free to create as many sliders as you would like per workbook and per column, though multiple sliders will simply overrule one another other if there are multiple per column. If you wish to delete the slicer that you created, simply click the X located in the top right corner of the slicer and it will disappear.

Slicers are highly customizable and come in 14 different pre-defined color schemes. By default, these themes are tied to the theme color you've chosen for your desktop and update accordingly. It is also possible to create your own theme if you are so inclined. To do so, simply select the button labeled New Style which can be found in the style gallery for slicers.

Additional adjustable preferences include the size of the slicer, as well as its layout, position and whether or not the slicer appears when the workbook is printed. These extra options can be found by first right-clicking on a particular slicer and then selecting the option for Properties. This is also where you can find the option to give the slicer a name and/or a description. Finally, the Settings option will allow you to name the slicer for formula purposes, provide a caption for the slicer and determine how it filters the table it affects.

Personalized List Sorting
Data can also be sorted by using a number of custom lists that come preinstalled and ready to go with most spreadsheet programs. They allow you to automatically sort data based on things like what day of the week it refers to or by the month the data was entered.

To use this feature, select the cells you wish to organize, visit the Data tab and select the Sort option. From there you will find what you are looking for under the Column heading, where you will find a box labeled Sort By which will provide you with all of the possible sorting options. Additional options can be found under custom lists; you can even create your own. Ensure each column you are sorting has a column heading for best results.

Chapter 7: Pivot Tables

Pivot tables are an easy way to concisely compare large amounts of data. Your spreadsheet program is good about recognizing the need for pivot tables and, assuming your settings allow it, will recommend the use of and automatically create pivot tables if you let it, helping you to present, explore, analyze and summarize your data as efficiently as possible. Before attempting to create a pivot table it is important that you ensure all of your columns and tables have headings and that they are all free of unprintable characters/blank cells or extra spaces.

To insert a pivot table, begin by selecting a single cell that exists in the table or range of cells. From there, head to the Insert tab and then choose the option to let the spreadsheet recommend pivot tables. This will then open a new dialog box which will suggest a variety of pivot tables that could be made with your current data, chose the one you want and the spreadsheet will create it as soon as you provide consent. Pivot tables can be deleted by simply selecting the pivot table in question and pressing the delete key. If you get an error message in response, ensure the complete pivot table has been selected and try again.

Field List
After the pivot table has been created, the field list will automatically appear to let you filter your data to a greater degree of specificity. The field list can also be found under the tab labeled Pivot Table Tools. This will provide you with a list of available fields you can add to a specific table as well as a

section of four boxes one for values, rows, columns and filters. Relevant fields cam be switched between the various boxes as need requires.

Most commonly, fields that don't contain numbers are added to rows while numerals are typically added into the values sections and things like specific dates or times are placed in the columns area. Fields can be removed from areas with the Remove Field Option.

Fields placed in the filters area will appear above the pivot table and act as filters for the entire table. Fields in the columns area appear at the top of the pivot table. Depending on the specifics, columns can also be found nested inside other columns. Rows are found at the left of the pivot table and can be nestled inside one another when there is a need for it. Values can be found beneath columns and are typically summarized and shown as numeric values. Multiple fields in a given area can be sorted by dragging them to their desired positions.

Sort your pivot tables
Pivot tables offer several easy options for simple sorting including arrows directly on the list of columns and rows, this will allow you to sort both in descending or ascending order. These arrows will also allow you to access additional value or label filters, remove fields or access additional options for sorting. Columns which do not automatically have arrows included can also be sorted by choosing a cell in the row or column, right-clicking on it and then selecting the Sort option.

When sorting pivot tables, it is important to keep in mind the fact that data which contains leading spaces is likely to affect the results as they are being sorted. As such, it is important to remove these leading spaces before sorting the data. Also, remember that text sensitive entries cannot be sorted and you are limited in the types of sorting you can use which means no sorting by font color, cell color, format or other conditional types of formatting.

Analyzing external data using a pivot table
If you need to analyze data that is stored someplace besides the spreadsheet program you are using, it is surprising easy to create a pivot table using that data as long as the external information is stored in an Online Analytical Processing cube file, a server database or in Microsoft Access.

- Start by choosing a cell in the worksheet you want the external data to end up in eventually.

- Choose the tab labeled Insert, followed by the option to create a pivot table.

- From the resulting dialogue box, find the option for selecting the type of data you wish to use, from there you will be present with an option to select a source of data to be accessed externally.

- You will now be able to determine the type of connection which will depend on the type of external source you are using. If you have used this process before, the Connections in this Workbook option will provide you with previously used connections.

- The tab labeled Other Sources will allow you to pull information using either an SQL Server or Analysis Services.

- Access databases can be found under the Data tab by selecting the From Access option. From there select the option for Data Source and select the Open option. You will then be able to choose the information you want to use. Note, ensure the option for multiple tables is checked if you plan on using multiple files.

- Chose where you would like the resulting pivot table to be placed, it can be placed into either a new or existing worksheet.

- After finalizing your choices, an empty pivot table should appear followed by the field list with a further list of specifics based on your imported data.

- Data models (chapter 11) can also be imported into pivot tables by selecting the option for an external data source before selecting the Choose Connection option followed by the Tables tab.

- The This Workbook Data Model option will provide you with the data you need to create a pivot chart.

Create a pivot table from more than one existing table
Relational data can easily be shown in a pivot table simply by grouping common values together. In these instances, the field list will show all of the

tables you can you show in the pivot table. The fields from each of these tables can then be placed onto the table at your discretion. To use multiple tables from the same workbook you will first need to create a relationship between the two tables.

- It is important that both tables have a column which can in turned be mapped to one of the columns from the other table. Ensure this column only contains unique information and both tables are named.

- Select the Data tab and the option for Relationships and then the New option.

- Select the option for the base table which the other table or tables will then be linked to.

- In the Column Foreign option choose the column that is relevant for the relationship.

- Select the table and column that you then want to relate to the first table and column in the Related Table/Column sections. Confirm your choices.

- Creating your pivot table should now result in multiple tables being visible on the pivot table field list option.

Alter pivot table source data

Once a pivot table has been created, the range of data it uses for its source can be easily altered based on your needs.

- Clicking on the pivot table you wish to alter will bring up the list of tools for use with the pivot table.

- Under the Data tab, select the Analyze option followed by Change Data Source.

- Select the new range you will want to use in the box labeled Table/Range. Instead of typing the new information, simply select it on your worksheet and it should auto populate this section.

- If your external data source has changed, this can be reflected from the same menu by selecting the external data source option.

- Pivot tables based on data models cannot be changed.

- Like regular tables, pivot tables can be refreshed by clicking on the pivot table you wish to refresh to bring up the tools for use with the pivot table, select the Data tab followed by the option to Analyze, then Refresh or Refresh all to refresh every pivot table in your workbook at once. You can also press the ALT key in conjunction with F5.

- When altering data ensure you prevent columns and cells from reformatting incorrectly by first selecting the Data tab followed by the option to Analyze and then Options. Select the tab labeled Layout and Format and ensure that the options for column width and cell formatting are selected.

Chapter 8: Make the Most of Macros

Macros can be used to save you time on a wide variety of tasks that you would otherwise have to perform manually. A macro is essentially a group of commands strung together to automatically perform one specific goal. Macros can be written using the programing language known as Visual Basic, but an easier way to set them up is to use what is known as the macro recorder.

The macro recorder lets you store a series of steps to be strung together as a single command. The macro recorder remembers everything you do; ensure you practice all of the steps you want the macro to perform before you start recording. While not naturally available, the macro recorder can be accessed by first turning on the Developer tab.

- Start by choosing the tab label File before selecting Options.

- In the resulting dialogue box, select the option to Customize Ribbon before choosing the Developer option which can be found in the Main Tabs section of the window on the right side of the window. Confirming your selection will make the Developer tab show up on the primary ribbon.

Edit the Personal Macro Workbook
To edit macros which are part of the Personal Macro Workbook file you must first take the extra step of making this file viewable.

- Start from the Home tab by choosing the Cells group

- Choose the Formatting option.

- Find the option for hiding things and choose what you need from the resulting list.

Record a macro
- Select the tab labeled Developer after enabling it using the steps suggested at the beginning of the chapter before choosing the Record Macros option from the grouping of options found above Code.

- In the resulting box, add the name of the macro you are creating. Take note, Macro names have to start with a letter and they are not allowed to uses spaces or reference cells directly. The name you enter will not be case sensitive.

- After setting the name of the macro you will be asked to give it a keyboard shortcut. If you assign it to an already existing shortcut, the new shortcut will replace the old but only in the workbook that the macro is saved too.

- You will then be provided with an option to store the macro in a variety of locations including the current workbook, a new workbook or the personal macro workbook which is useful if you wish to have access to the macro you create whenever you use the spreadsheet program regardless of what specific workbook you are using.

- You will then be given the opportunity to add a description to your macro before confirming all of your choices to begin the recording process.

- After you have confirmed your choices you will immediately begin recording the macro in question so it is important to be prepared. Steps you take will be recorded exactly and references you make to cells will be record precisely.

- If you want the macro to instead use relative references (for example, up one cell and over two instead of Cell A1) there is a button for them specifically on the Developer tab which can be switched on and off as needed throughout the recording process.

- Selecting the stop option will prevent any more keystrokes from being recorded and stores and saves the macro which is immediately ready for use. The stop button should be visible at the bottom of the screen for the duration of the recording.

- Once they have been recorded, macros can be run using a shortcut you set during their generation or by pressing the ALT key in conjunction with the F8 key to bring up a list of available macros for the current workbook. You then select the macro you wish to run and select the run option.

Use VBA to make a macro
- Ensure the developer tab is being displayed using the steps suggested at the beginning of the chapter before selecting Macro Security

from the grouping of options listed above Code.

- Select the Settings options before choosing to enable all macros. Ignore the warning but ensure you return the settings to where they started when you are done to prevent harmful code from infecting your computer.

- With that finished, select the Visual Basic option, also from the Developers tab and the Code grouping.

- This will bring up the editor for Visual Basic, choose the menu labeled Insert and the option for Module. Take note, this will create a shortcut for all workbooks in the spreadsheet program. Besides macros, class modules, userforms and regular modules can be created from this window.

- One of the windows you can access from the Visual Basics Editor is what is known as the Project Window which will show you all of the current VBA macros which are currently operating in the selected workbook

- Now it is time to add the code for the macro you want to use, to ensure it works properly hit F5 to watch it run while still in this window. Be sure to note that the VBA features available in the spreadsheet program are relatively limited which means they cannot contain calls to procedures, functions which are built in, loops, IF statements, arrays, variables or defined constants.

- After you have finished writing your macro, select the option to close and return to your spreadsheet from the File menu.

Add a macro to another macro
- Ensure the Developer tab is being displayed using the steps suggested at the beginning of the chapter before selecting Macro Security from the grouping of options above Code.

- Select the Settings options before choosing to enable all macros. Ignore the warning but ensure you return the settings to where they started when you are done to prevent harmful code from infecting your computer.

- With this completed, find the workbook which contains the macro you wish to copy before opening the Macro option on the Developer tab in the group of options above the Code group.

- From the available list of macros, choose the one you wish to use to make a copy before selecting the option to Edit. The code you want to copy will now be available in the Visual Basic Editor.

- If you want to use the entirety of the macro you have selected it is important that you copy the part of the code in the Sub line and End Sub sections.

- With the code selected, go to the menu labeled Edit and choose the Copy option or press the CTRL key in conjunction with the C key.

- Find the box labeled Procedure, also in the code window, here you will find the list of modules where you can place the code. Once you have found where to place the code, choose the Paste option from the Edit menu or press the CRTL key in conjunction with the V key.

Give a control, graphic or object its own macro
If you wish to assign a macro to a specific control, graphic or object the macro must already exist beforehand. Once it has been created using the steps listed above:
- Start by right-clicking on the control, graphic or object you wish to assign the macro to.

- Choose the option to Assign Macro from the resulting menu before selecting the macro you wish to assign and confirm your decision.

Remove a macro
Macros can be deleted easily assuming you have the Developer tab enabled using the steps suggested at the beginning of the chapter. If the macro you are looking to delete is in the Personal Macro Workbook, ensure you unhide it using the steps suggested at the beginning of the chapter.
- Start by selecting the workbook which holds the macro scheduled for deletion.

- Use the Developers tab to find the Macros options which can be found under the grouping of options in the Code area.

- From there you will be given a list of macros which can be deleted.

- Choose the macro and confirm your choice.

Chapter 9: Modeling Management

A data model will provide you with the opportunity to use data from multiple tables in a new way. They provide relational data which can be exported to other workbooks, providing transparency and tabular data results which can then be imported into pivot tables, charts and reports made with Power View. Each workbook can only have a single data model at a time but one data model can be used on multiple worksheets simultaneously. The workbook data model can be found by looking under External Data Sources in the Pivot table menu under the Tables option.

In your spreadsheet program these models are natively shown as tables which can be manipulated with a field list; to view them in their true form however, you will need to download what is known as the Microsoft Office Power Pivot add-in for the version of the spreadsheet program you are currently using. To find this add-on, visit Support.Office.com and search for the version of the add-on for the version of the spreadsheet program you are using.

Data created using Power Pivot is stored in a separate database inside your spreadsheet program which allows it to access an internal search engine for queries and updates that load more quickly than other parts of your spreadsheet program. This data is spread between pivot charts, pivot table and Power View. This data can also be shared remotely through the use of the SharePoint server.

Once you have downloaded the add-on you still need to activate it as part of your spreadsheet program. To enable it:

- Select the tab labeled File follow by Options, then Add-ins

- Look for the box labeled manage before choosing COM Add-ins and then Go.

- Look for the box labeled Microsoft Office Power Pivot and check the box marked OK.

- If you followed the steps correctly, you should now see a separate tab labeled Power Pivot in your main ribbon.

If you choose to import data that is relational, a data model will automatically be created at the point multiple tables are selected. To do this:

- In your spreadsheet program, select the option for Data followed by Get External Data to bring in data from an external source which contains multiple tables.

- The next window will allow you to select a table, as you want to select multiple tables, ensure the box to allow you to do so is checked before choosing your tables selecting next and then Finish.

- Select the option you want in relation to the way the data will be visualized. This will create the data model that you can then manipulate later. This model will be updated automatically as you manipulate the worksheet. When you rename a table after this step has been completed you will need to resync the data model by repeating the previous steps.

Prevent the data model from automatically syncing changes
Data models are linked to their related pivot tables by default, this can be changed from any worksheet which uses the data model in question.

- In a worksheet which is using the data model in question, select the Power Pivot tab to open the Power Pivot options menu.

- In the bottom row of tabs, you should see a list of the tables you are using, the linked tables will have an icon near their names.

- In the resulting ribbon, choose the Linked Table option.

- In the resulting menu, find the option for Update Mode and select the Manual option. To update the data mode in while in manual, look for the Update options in the ribbon for Linked Tables.

Add to a data model
After you have created a data model it is possible to add disparate data to it, this process works best with data that is named.

- Select the data that needs to be added to the model or, if the data is a named range simply select a cell in that range.

- Choose the tab for Power Pivot before selecting the option to add an additional Data Model.

- Choose the Insert tab followed by the Pivot Table option. Ensure the dialogue box allowing you to add data to already modeled data is checked.

- The additional data has now been added to the data model in the form of a linked table.

Extend or refine data models
In the traditional spreadsheet interface, data models are presented as pivot tables to maximize ease of analysis and data exploration. If you instead wish to interact with the data model more directly by removing specific tables or fields, view all of the data that makes up the model directly, add business logic, hierarchies or KPIs then the Power Pivot add-in is what you are looking for. Additional data model optimizations include deciding on a field list that populates by default, icons or images to represent certain columns or rows. To use Power Pivot:

- Select the Power Pivot tab before choosing the Manage option.

- The resulting window will show you all of the optimizations that you can apply to the current data model.

- Certain types of visualizations will only work with certain types of data.

Gathering Data with Power Pivot
Once you get used to it, you will find that determining relational data is much faster using the Power Pivot add-in than using traditional methods. The benefits of importing data this way

include the ability to remove data that doesn't relate to the model, rename things as you import them or use otherwise predefined terms to find related data to import. This will also save you steps when it comes to creating new relationships as every table that is imported into Power Pivot will automatically have its relevant relationships tagged.

- Select the Power Pivot tab followed by Home, Get External Data and then finally choosing the From Database choice assuming the data you are looking for is dimensional or relational.

- Other sources can be found using the Suggest related Data Option under the Data Service option found on the Home tab of Power Pivot.

- Data that you select can either be imported whole cloth or the data can be filtered by choosing specific view or tables or writing a list of what you want to be imported.

- Data used in the model can be refreshed from the Power Pivot tab by selecting the Data option then Connections and then Refresh All. This refresh works by looking for the original data that was imported and seeking to import it again. Data will disappear if the required connections can't be made.

- Data from almost every type of source is supported with the exception of published server documents.

When using this method, it is important to keep in mind that OLE DB options will almost always work more quickly when it comes to scaling large amounts of data. Always look for OLE DB options when they are available.

Common issues
If your Power Pivot tab stops appearing when you open your spreadsheet program this might be because your spreadsheet program has decided that the add-on is causing the program to become unstable. This is typically caused if the spreadsheet program crashes while the Power Pivot window is active. To restore the missing tab:

- Select the tab labeled File followed by Options and then Add-ins

- Look for the box labeled Manage then the option for Disable Items

- Choose Go then look for the option for Microsoft Office Power Pivot and set the selection to Enable.

- If the same issue keeps occurring, then start by closing out of your spreadsheet program.

- Open the start menu and select the run option before typing into the resulting box regedit.

- After the registry editor opens look for the registry key that relates to User Settings for your version of the spreadsheet program.

- Look for the listing called PowerPivotExcelAddin, right-click on it and choose delete.

- Return to the beginning of the Registry Editor and look for the spreadsheet program Addins string.

- Look for the PowerPivotExcelClientAddIn.NativeEntry.1 and right-click to delete it.

- Close the editor and reopen the spreadsheet program before following the original instructions for enabling Power Pivot.

Chapter 10: Power View

If you are already using pivot tables to create data models and Power Pivot to manipulate your data models, then Power View is the final piece of the puzzle. It can be used to present and visualize your data models in reports that are like no other. Power View can easily take any type of data and use it to form bar charts, pie charts, even bubble charts. Matrices and complex tables can even be automatically broken down into multiple charts. Power View is only available for versions of the spreadsheet program going back to 2013. If your company uses Microsoft Power BI, then Power View is also available.

Power View sheets can be created from the Insert Tab by selecting the Power View option and they will automatically detect your current data model. Your version of the spreadsheet program may not have Power View enabled by default if this is the case, follow the steps listed below:

- Choose File, then Options, followed by Customize Ribbon.

- Select the option for Main Tabs, then select where you wish the Power View option to appear.

- Select the option to add additional commands followed by commands that are not found in the ribbon and then choose the option to Insert Power View.

- Selected the option to add, then choose where you want to find the Power View option, before naming the new group.

- After confirming your choices, you will still need to activate the add-in for Power View. To do this, you will need to click on the Power View option you create on your ribbon before choosing the option to enable when prompted to do so.

Creating a Power View Sheet

- Creating a Power View Sheet after you have activated Power View option on the ribbon is as easy as clicking the button on the ribbon.

- This will then provide you with a list of options regarding tables which can be visualized. Selecting a table will provide you with a list of options that Power View has determined will provide the message of the data most clearly.

- The Design tab can be used to alter the current visualization.

Filter data in Power View

Power View can filter data based on the metadata provided from the data model as a baseline to understand the relationships between the data in the model. The filter options can be found on the Filter pane and provides options to cross-filters and slicers as well as standard filters. This is also where the option to highlight specific portions of the data can be found. These options can be applied to the entirety of the current Power View sheet or just certain portions of the data.

These filters can be applied in real time, simply by selecting certain portions of the data that is being presented. To filter data simply click on it and see what happens. For example, choosing a specific column may automatically filter the display to show all the variations on that specific type of data or highlight for additional emphasis. Pressing the CTRL key in addition to clicking on a value will allow you to select additional values. Clicking on a filter, not a value, will reset the display.

Power Pivot and Power View Interaction
If you know you plan on using Power View with the data model, you are improving using Power Pivot then there are a few things you can do to make the transition from one to another as smooth as possible.

- Ensure you have chosen the correct default aggregation. The spreadsheet program defaults to Sum for this sort of thing, to change this open the Power Pivot tab and choose the Manage option. Choose the tables you wish to change and set your cursor on the column to provide you access with the Advanced tab. Choose the desired aggregation from the resulting options menu.

- Ensure you have always chosen the identifiers, images and titles for all of your data model tables.

Power View default field

Set a default field for Power View sheets which will allow certain fields to be automatically added to Power View based on need. By activating this feature, you can have new information added to the data model simply by selecting predefined tables.

- Open the workbook which houses the data model you wish to use before selecting the Power Pivot tab and the Properties option.

- Choose the table you wish to add a default list to.

- Select the Advanced option followed by Default Field Set.

- Choose the fields from the table you wish to add automatically before selecting the Add option.

- These fields will be added to the model in order, and can be rearranged from this screen.

- If done correctly, clicking on a table while in Power View will cause it to auto-populate the fields you have selected.

Conclusion Excel for Business

Thank you again for purchasing this book! I hope this book was able to help you to learn more about many of the more advanced features that your spreadsheet program has to offer. While some of the steps outlined above seem as though they would be cumbersome, over time you will find they speed up many of the common tasks you regularly perform.

The next step is to stop reading already and start practicing the techniques that you feel will be most useful to your everyday life. Don't stop there however, you will be surprised how useful all of the above techniques can be, give the ones you don't think you will need a try as well and see what happens. Remember, proper spreadsheet usage is a skill and like any other skill it only improves with practice.

Finally, if you enjoyed this book, then I'd like to ask you for a favor, would you be kind enough to leave a review for this book on Amazon? It'd be greatly appreciated!

Bibliography

Francesco Iannello, born in Italy in 1982, is an Information Technology lecturer, professional Web Designer, Social Media Manager and Data Analyst.

Thanks to a hands-on approach education as programmer and long-lasting experiences in big companies, he has developed strong training and communication skills that have enabled him to hold courses, seminars and academic lessons aimed at different audiences.

He has mastered in the strategic usage of the calc spreadsheet and its application to create forecasts, monitoring and business modelings and in the application of the LEAN method in big production companies.

Currently, he is the official supplier of IULM University of Milan of communication services, responsible for Social Media campaigns and the production of communication materials.

Follow Me

- ✓ LinkedIn
- ✓ Google+
- ✓ Facebook
- ✓ Twitter
- ✓ Pinterest
- ✓ Telegram

FMT

Fast Memorization Techniques

Accelerated Learning Advanced Technique for Fast Learning

Author

Joe Bronski

Disclaimer

perceived slight of any individual or organization is purely unintentional.

Introduction Extra Bonus

Have you ever wondered what the difference between you and someone who seems to able to endlessly spout facts they have memorized? Or while you were in school why others just seemed to have a much easier time remember facts for tests or were always getting better scores then you? Though some people are just naturally gifted learners the odds are they were taught techniques you were not exposed to and has given them the ability to better retain the information they were taught. They also most likely practiced their techniques keeping their mind sharp and making retention all the easier for their efforts.

There are so many techniques out there for memorization and learning. Some are more effective then others and they all depend on the type of learner you are. This book has been put together to help cover some of the more advanced memorization techniques that can be utilized. Most learning is considered the tradition approach with the student in a more passive role and the teacher will actively put knowledge before the student in an attempt to help them retain the information.

While this has had some success in the past, research has revealed that an accelerated learning approach helps a learner retain more information faster than the tradition techniques. This style encourages the student to become an active participant in their learning as well as helping them truly manipulate the material allowing for total retention in a shorter timeframe. It also allows them to have a much greater grasp of the material because they are forced to place it in their own words and manipulate the information in a way that allows their brain to better understand the concepts they are learning.

This book will go over these techniques in some detail in the hope of helping you become faster and more efficient at memorizing important information. There are different aspects of material that help to determine how difficult it is to study. Theses properties will be discussed as well as strategies that can be used to improve how effectively you can memorize those types of material. We will discuss ways in which you can properly prepare your body for memorization and give you the best chances at retaining the information. It is also believed that seeking a few other sources before you begin your studying can help you give a broader picture and better understanding of what your learning.

Hopefully with the information you are given here, you will be able to efficiently and more completely memorize information that you need to retain. Remember working with your mind is just like working any other muscle in your body. You need to consistently work with it to strengthen the muscle. By applying some of these techniques as well as practicing everyday just like you would if you were an athlete you will be able to better improve your abilities to memorize and retain.

Chapter 1: Why Memorization is Difficult and How to Help Yourself

With research it has been determined that there are about 11 characteristics of information that determine how difficult or easy something is to memorize. Armed with the knowledge of these various characteristics you will hopefully be able to identify why certain knowledge it easier to retain while you struggle in other areas. After you have been given these characteristics will go over strategies that can help you improve memorization with information containing the various characteristics.

- ✓ Abstractness, this characteristic refers to how easy it is to wrap your head around the concept. If the concept is abstract in a nature it will be harder to relate to and make it all the more difficult to put into terms that you will be able to easily understand. The harder an object is to understand the more difficult it is to remember.

- ✓ Complexity, how complex or difficult a problem is can certainly determine how difficult it can be to retain. The more intricate the information the harder it will be for your mind to remember everything in its proper place.

✓ Familiarity, is how much exposure you have had to the information you are trying to retain. If you are memorizing information on something you interact with on a day to day basis it will be easier to remember information about it.

✓ Humanness, this characteristic refers to how relatable a subject is to the human experiences in life. The more relevance a subject has to being human or experiences we face as human beings the easier it is to relate to and retain.

✓ Immediacy, how soon information needs to be retained. The shorter the time frame that information needs to be memorized by the harder or easier it can be to retain depending on your personality.

✓ Importance, this characteristic points to how much the information you are trying to memorize impacts your life. The more important it can be to your life in any way can make it easier to remember.

✓ Order, the more logical the structure of the information the easier it will be to retain. The more convoluted the information and the harder to decipher its proper order the more difficult it will be for you to remember. Our minds immediately seek to make things easier for us to understand, so if the order doesn't make sense it will be harder for our brains to retain.

✓ Relevance, the more useful information will be to you the easier it will be to retain. If its something you can use in your everyday life or can help you in your endeavors the odds are it will be easier to memorize.

✓ Salience, when we find information boring it makes it that much harder to focus on the subject. When your bored in class you fall asleep, a similar thing can happen to your brain. When it's bored it can fall asleep in a sense and make it more difficult to retain what your attempting to.

✓ Sensuous, how your senses receive the information you want to learn will help to determine how much easier it is to retain. If you can sense it on more planes it is more likely you will be able to remember it.
✓ Size, this characteristic can easily be seen as one that helps determine your retention of something. The more their is to retain the more difficult it can be.

Now that we have talked about how these characteristics affect how easy or hard it can be to retain information we will go over ways in which you can improve in areas you might struggle in. If you add characteristics to the material you are trying to retain and you discover a pattern to the types of material you struggle with then you can use these tips to hopefully help you overcome your shortcomings in that retention area.

- ✓ Abstractness, try to relate the information to what's around you. If you can find a way to make it less abstract and easier to relate to the everyday it will be that much easier to remember.

- ✓ Complexity, if you break it down into smaller pieces or simpler steps it can make it easier to understand and retain.

- ✓ Familiarity, try to review information more frequently. If you can try to review it for a short amount of time every day. The more you are exposed to it the more familiar you will be with it.

- ✓ Humanness, turn your information in a story and try to make yourself the main character. Not only will it help you relate the information to something more natural. By making yourself the star it will be all the more interesting to remember.

✓ Immediacy, setting yourself a deadline to have information retained by can help keep you motivated even if you don't need it for any particular time. Sometimes if you don't need it for a test or something similar you may procrastinate on the material in question.

✓ Importance, try to set a goal or objective to memorizing the information. If you can make it more important to yourself, it will be easier to retain.

✓ Order, if you struggle to remember information and the order makes no sense simply restructure it in a way that makes sense to you. You will then be able to better retain the information.

✓ Relevance, if you figure out a way in which it can be relevant to your life it will make it easier to retain.

✓ Salience, try to create a story to go along with the information. If you can string the information together in a funny or crazy way it will not only be more memorable but it will keep it more interesting.

✓ Sensuous, if you can only associate your information with one sense you may find it harder to retain but if you try to find other sense that it can relate to you will find it easier to remember. It may take a little creativity to figure out how to engage other senses but it can be a big help.

✓ Size, if you have a large amount of material to cover break it down into smaller chunks to give your brain a more manageable chunk of information to remember.

When memorizing information most people use familiarity in order to retain information. Others who are better at retaining information.

Chapter 2: Preparing Your Body

One of the most important things you can do to help you become a memorization wiz is to take care of yourself. By ensuring that your system is running at its best you will give your mind the best shot possible to retain information. A body that is sleep deprived or not given the proper fuel will not function as well as one that is. So by following a few of these simple steps you will set your mind up for success and making learning and retaining what you have learned that much easier.

Get enough sleep, it cannot be stressed enough how important sleep is. Try to get at least 7 hours of sleep a day, a well rested mind is more prepared to retain information and is just more ready to work in general. Also minimize your blue light exposure before going to sleep, so avoid computers, your phones, and TV before bed.

Try to keep yourself well hydrated. If you can keep water or maybe even some unsweetened tea, sugar will defeat the exercise, your body and brain will be able to better function getting the water that it needs to live off of.

Sugar can be your enemy in the case of studying, it may seem like a great jolt to keep you going but the crash can stop you in your tracks and make things worse for you. The excess energy can be the wrong kind making your more fidgety then able to sit and focus like you may need to.

Walk or exercise on a regular basis if you can. The better your body function the healthier you will feel and your brain will feel. You are also more likely to feel happier and better about yourself and this lift in mood can make focusing and studying that much easier.

Try to avoid stressors and schedule out your day to a certain degree so you can reach optimal productivity during your day. Not only will you feel like you have accomplished something it will help keep you from stressing about things you need to accomplish because you will already be preparing your   brain.

Chapter 3: A Few Other Techniques

In this day and age there are far too many distractions available to take our attention away from the tasks at hand. But if you would like to be able to memorize information faster and become a better learner there are a few techniques you can employ to help you double or even triple the amount of information you can retain in your sessions. When you allow yourself to be distracted you make it that much harder for your brain to simple take in the information you are presenting it. With those other distractions joking for the position of attention in your mind it will force you to work that much harder to try and remember.

If you are a music lover try to listen to music without lyrics. Music with lyrics can interfere with your language processing abilities. So when you listen to music with lots of lyrics you're essentially sabotaging yourself. Your brain will be unable to totally focus on one set of information because the other will either be spoken or read and disrupt the flow of the other. So instead try to listen to music that is only instrumental. If you can stay away from music that has any lyrics your can still listen to sounds in the background without distracting yourself from the material and make learning and retention that much easier.

Try to choose times that are most conducive to studying. If you choose to work when you are very likely to be interrupted, you will easily be distracted with each interruption and make it that much harder for yourself. Also shoot for times with your have energy. If you are tired your mind is likely to be clear and able to engage in the types of mental gymnastics you are asking of it. You would never ask you body to run a marathon when you are exhausted so why ask the same of your brain? It is a muscle too. By keeping distractions to a minimum and being properly energized you are also less likely to experience stress while studying which can also make it easier on yourself. The more stressed you are the harder it will be to concentrate on the task at hand.

With the technology available to us it can be extremely hard to disconnect from everything and everyone around us. By having a cellphone, you are totally accessible to everyone at all times. This constant connection can be so distracting, talking with your friends or finding out what someone just posted on Facebook can be so much more engaging then the studying you are trying to accomplish. But if you want to be able to memorize and retain the information you are working with you need to do yourself a favor and unplug from everything around you. Turn off notifications, your cell phone, whatever you need to do to be totally focused on the task at hand. This can be very hard for some people especially if they have never done it before. If this is the case for you try for about 20 minutes at a time. You don't want to drive yourself to distraction by being unplugged because that wont achieve anything either.

Many people studying sitting or laying down. While this restful state can help keep you focused on one thing and one thing only you also don't want to completely sit like a lump the whole time. Standing and walking around for short breaks can help promote blood flow and even energy into your body. Both are helpful for keeping you fresh and focused. You also provide more oxygen to your brain from the increased blood flow and the more oxygen your brain has the better it will function.

Prioritize the material you are about to review. If say you feel very confident on certain parts of the information you are cover then you should skip those parts and review what you are shakier with. When you go over material you are already very familiar with you can give yourself a false sense of security. You will feel like you know more and take time away from the information that really needs your attention. It will also increase your exposure to what you are unfamiliar with helping you to each maximum retention of all the topics you are trying to remember.

Tell yourself a story. This is one that can't be stressed enough, if you can find a story to help show you the information you are trying to learn that's excellent and you should read it. But if you can make one up, by placing information into a relatable story your brain will have an easier time remember that then trying to chock down random bits of information. Telling your story to someone else or even attempting to teach them material will also help you to better retain it. When you teach someone else you are forced to reword the information and put it into each to understand bites for someone who doesn't know the material. This rewording and forcing you to really work with the concepts will give you a better understanding and make it that much easier to understand.

The last tip to keep in mind is to try and preview the content you are about to go over. By going on other websites or searching in other books before getting down to some serious studying or memorization you can help to give yourself perspective on material that might not necessarily be clear from the source you are currently reading. It can make things clearer it can also give you different perspective that can help the information to click in your mind and help you to remember it better. You can also give yourself a bigger picture if you skim before you read in detail. You will better be able to see where the text is heading and hopefully by causing that light of recognition in your brain you will be reinforcing some pathways in your brain.

Conclusion Extra Bonus

Thank you for purchasing this book. There is a lot of information out there just waiting to be retained for you to use later or apply to your everyday life. So why would you want to wait or let everything that there is to learn out their pass you by? The world is full of so much knowledge and now with some of the techniques in this book anyone can start memorizing information like a pro.

Try to work through all the techniques in this book and don't forget about a few life style changes you can make to help improve your health and your mind. You can neglect one part of yourself and still expect to get the same results so remember to give all parts a try to get the best results possible.

It is our hope that you were able to get all the information you could need from this book and we hope that you will share your experiences with others. By reviewing this book not only will you be helping others with their decisions you will also being giving us invaluable feedback to help us keep improving any more information we try to provide in the future. Your feedback is so important to us and we value your opinion as our avid customer.

Enter your Work Notes: